Second Edition

D1408070

Coaching
Defensive Linemen

John Levra
James A. Peterson

★★★★★
COACHES
≡ **CHOICE**™

ISBN: 978-1-58518-064-6
Library of Congress Control Number: 20077936328
Book layout and cover design: Roger W. Rybkowski
Diagrams: Marion von Bausler and Roger W. Rybkowski

Coaches Choice
P.O. Box 1828
Monterey, CA 93942
www.coacheschoice.com

Dedication

I want to dedicate this book to every member of my wonderful family. Without their guidance and support, coaching would have been impossible. My mom and dad, Mildred and Pete Levra, provided so much for me as a young man. My wife, Rosie, and our children, Craig and Gina, have been with me every season, no matter what the outcome of our games. Their love, patience, and understanding could not have been any better. Collectively, their backing has enabled me to continue to pursue my goals in the profession, and lead a very rewarding life while enjoying the game of football.

—John Levra

Acknowledgments

I would like very much to thank all of the outstanding coaches I have had the opportunity to work with during my career for their expert advice and counsel. Each of them taught me a lot about coaching—in particular, about defensive line play. The list of coaches who have had a positive impact on enabling me to better learn my craft is quite extensive. Among the high school coaches who helped me professionally were Bill Presson, Bob Hughes, and Chuck Norris. On the college level, I thoroughly enjoyed working with Jack Scofield, Mart Crawford, Lance Van Zandt, Cliff Silva, Dick Munzinger, Lloyd Moore, Jerry Moore, and Bud Moore. Among the coaches at the professional level who willingly shared their insights and knowledge with me are Vic Rapp, Vince Tobin, Bum Phillips, Wade Phillips, Carl Mauck, Mike Ditka, Dave McGinnis, Jim Fassel, Dennis Green, Tony Dungy, Foge Fazio, King Hill, John Paul Young, Andy Everest, Jim La Rue, Tom Olivadotti, and Joe Spencer.

I would also like to express my appreciation to all of the great defensive linemen that I've had the privilege of coaching (including Richard Dent, Steve McMichael, Dan Hampton, William "The Fridge" Perry, Trace Armstrong, and John Randle), who were more than willing to share the "little" things that helped me to improve my ability to teach the defensive line position.

I would also like to acknowledge my junior high coaches (Estel Gilmour), high school coaches (Harry McDonald, Sam Nicoletti, Lefty Hamm), and college coaches (Carnie Smith, Joe Murphy), all of whom helped inspire me to choose coaching as a career. I am very thankful for both their guidance and their teachings. They were great teachers and coaches.

I would also like to extend my appreciation to Kristi Huelsing and Alisha Brown for their patience and assistance in guiding me through the editorial process. Finally, I would like to thank Jim Peterson, my co-author, who convinced me that I had something of value to say and offer to coaches. He did a great job of putting the manuscript together.

—John Levra

Contents

Preface

Over the years, the game of football has changed in a number of ways. The players—in many instances—have gotten bigger and faster. To a great extent, the offenses have become more varied and complex. In response, the defenses have attempted to become even more intricate and focused.

The one aspect of this great sport that has not changed in any meaningful way since its inception is the fact that the basic essence of the game is embodied in two fundamental activities—blocking and tackling. For many individuals, the resolute determination of a particular player of a specific team to overpower and control the competition defines the compelling nature of the sport.

Having coached on both sides of the line (offense and defense), I have an acute appreciation of the physical and technical skills that are required to play football at a highly competitive level. As such, I believe that I have a rightful obligation to share with other members of the football coaching community much of the information and insights that I have been able to amass in more than four decades of coaching.

Coaching Defensive Linemen, Second Edition, is a by-product of the fact that because other coaches have taken the time and energy to share their opinions and ideas with me at all stages of my coaching career, I feel that I should attempt to reciprocate both their generosity and their commitment to the game by writing this book. As such, *Coaching Defensive Linemen,* Second Edition, attempts to provide a straightforward, inclusive overview of all aspects involved in this critical facet of the game.

Not only does the book cover how to preselect those individuals who might be most predisposed to play the defensive line at an effective level, it also reviews (in detail) those techniques that a defensive lineman must perform as expected against either the run or the pass. One of the more unique features of the book is the comprehensive chapter on technique play against the most common blocking schemes. The book also includes a chapter on drills that can be used to develop and refine the skills and techniques required of a defensive lineman. Finally, the book presents a detailed method for evaluating the level of play by a defensive lineman during an actual game.

By design, I have attempted to make the information presented in *Coaching Defensive Linemen,* Second Edition, useful for coaches at all competitive levels. If this information enables you to be better prepared to coach the young men for whom you are responsible, then the effort to write this book will have been well worth the time.

—John Levra

Becoming a Defensive Lineman

Defensive linemen set the tempo for a defensive football team. A good defensive team has defensive linemen who attack the line of scrimmage and give 100 percent effort on every play. A successful defense has linemen who out-hit and out-tough the opponent. To accomplish these objectives, a defensive lineman must possess certain mental and physical qualities, including the following:

- *Quickness.* A defensive lineman must have the ability to get off the ball on the snap and immediately shed the blocker.
- *Toughness.* The defensive lineman must be mentally up to the task of experiencing continuous contact and defeating blocking schemes aimed to control, frustrate, and discourage him (e.g., triple-teams, double-teams, false keys, etc.).
- *Speed.* The ability to accelerate to the ball once the blocker is shed is an indispensable requirement for a defensive lineman. Coaches should always keep in mind and remind their players that this attribute increases a defensive lineman's opportunity to be a "great" player.
- *Desire and determination.* A defensive lineman must possess an unrelenting commitment to perform at full throttle on every play (i.e., do his best) if he is to have any reasonable chance to excel.

- *Strength.* The defensive lineman must possess exceptional strength in both the upper and lower body that enables him to physically dominate the line of scrimmage.
- *Peripheral vision.* The defensive lineman must possess an extraordinary ability to see peripheral developments as the play progresses.
- *Stamina.* The defensive lineman must have the physical energy (e.g., aerobic capacity) to be able to defeat the blocker and relentlessly pursue the ball from sideline to sideline on each play from scrimmage.

Quickness and Speed

A strong argument can be made that quickness and speed in defensive linemen can eliminate many of the problems that a defensive line coach faces. The primary goal of an offensive lineman is to neutralize the pursuit of the defensive lineman. If a defensive lineman is a strong, but slow-footed athlete, his pursuit factor will be greatly diminished. The offensive lineman gains a significant advantage toward accomplishing his objective when he faces a slow defensive lineman.

Slow defensive linemen are unable to stretch the anchor zone of the defensive line of scrimmage. The anchor zone is that horizontal area that a defensive front can effectively control after the offensive-line charge is defeated. The faster the defensive lineman, the greater the anchor zone in which he is active. By the same token, the greater the anchor zone of the defensive front, the more effective the defense is against the run. Naturally, a faster athlete can increase the horizontal, or lateral, area of responsibility along the defensive line. This increase of lateral responsibility widens the defense's range of front control against the run. While a defensive line prospect with relatively slow foot speed may, in fact, be able to consistently anchor the point of attack between the tackles, he is at a distinct disadvantage in terms of controlling the required width of the anchor zone.

Another significant element of defensive line play that is closely related to the foot speed of an athlete is the pass rush. All factors considered, the effectiveness of the pass rush of a defensive lineman who is slow will be greatly reduced. The athlete must be fast enough to immediately close the distance to the pass protector, gain clearance past the blocker, and get to the quarterback as quickly as possible. The more favorable the speed differential between the pass protector and the pass rusher, the more pass-rushing moves that are available to the defensive lineman. To use his speed, the defensive lineman must be finely tuned to the movement of the football. The secret to becoming recognized as a great pass rusher is getting a consistent jump on the snap of the football.

Several physical coaching points can be used to enhance athletes' ability to take off on the ball, including the following:

- Throwing the hands on the snap of the ball
- Violently pushing off with the front foot
- Snapping the hips when throwing the body on the snap
- Pushing down on the knee with the up-hand
- Snatching the grass and clawing with the down-hand
- Replacing the down-hand with the back foot
- Leading with the nose, head, and shoulders
- Falling out of the stance

Desire and Determination

Defensive line play is always mentally intense, as well as physically demanding. It should be noted that the battle in the trenches is seldom (if ever) a shutout victory. The competition is such that even a very talented defensive lineman will lose some battles during the game. He may even lose the first battle on the first play from scrimmage. Eventually, however, the ability and the will to win of a highly talented defensive lineman will control play in the trenches. As such, defenders are able to maintain their poise and focus. All great defensive linemen play with a tenacious determination to whip the blocker and get to the football. Unrelenting tenacity and determination to make the play is the key component of the character makeup of a true warrior-type athlete in the trench.

Strength

A defensive lineman must be strong enough to grab the offensive lineman and establish physical dominance. Not only must a defensive lineman be able to grab the offensive lineman, but he must also be able to physically turn the offensive lineman's shoulders or throw him to one side. Leverage is the key word used in describing the proper use of strength to obtain an advantage over the offensive blocker. When discussing defensive line play and the physical techniques of play, neither strength nor leverage is independent of the other. The use of proper leverage without possessing adequate strength does not make for a complete defensive lineman. On the other hand, a defensive lineman who possesses superior strength but lacks the ability to perform the requisite techniques for gaining proper leverage is equally ineffectual.

Leverage refers to the angular strength of the total body. In particular, it involves the ability of a defender to lower his center of gravity to allow him to maintain a lower elevation and establish a lower anchor point on the blocker. Among the factors used to apply leverage are the following:

- Punching the heel of the hands to the blocking surface of the blocker. Normally, this surface is the blocker's chest and shoulders. On scramble blocks, or other blocks in which the blocker attempts to cut the legs of the defender, the blocking surface may be the backside of the shoulder or another posterior region of the blocker's upper body. In the case of maintaining leverage on the scramble block, the action of the feet, the flex of the hips, and the arm pressure on the blocker become even more significant aspects of the defender's response.
- Striking the opponent's chest near the outside edge of his jersey number.
- Using the fingers to grasp cloth, stabilize a surface, and form a pressure plate that the defender's arms may push against to gain separation.
- Whipping the blocker before looking for the ball. A common mistake among young linemen is looking over the top of the offensive lineman's pads. Defensive linemen must concentrate on the pads and the attack point and find the ball based on the blocking scheme.

Another advantage to having exceptional strength is the fact that possessing it can allow the defensive lineman to play in a more static manner on the line of scrimmage. In other words, the stronger the defensive lineman, the lesser the need to attack on the snap and read on the run. A defense that has a group of physically strong defensive linemen is able to employ a defensive scheme that controls the line of scrimmage and frees the linebackers to make plays from sideline to sideline. The term for holding two offensive linemen is "holding the jump through." In a reading defensive line play technique, the lineman will grab both blockers as they attempt to combo block or scoop block him and get up on the linebacker. If he can hold both of them, this perfect technique allows the linebacker to run to the ball.

When playing the static-control technique on the line of scrimmage, the defensive lineman responds to the movement of the offensive lineman, not the ball. The defender's objective is to stop the charge of the offensive lineman, anchor his gap, and slide down the line to either fill a cutback lane or become a member of the ball pursuit. His responsibility in widening his personal anchor zone is much more limited in the static-control scheme of play. When playing with this technique, the defensive front highlights the outstanding linebackers. The first-level defenders—the defensive linemen—use up the offensive blockers and allow the second-level defenders—the linebackers—to run unimpeded to the football. If a team has personnel who are capable of physically dominating the interior matchups along the line of scrimmage, the static-control style of defensive line play is the preferred tactic. As a rule, this control-and-anchor method is the method of line play used by teams who possess superior strength along the defensive line. It was the technique utilized by the great defensive line of the 1985 Super Bowl champions, the Chicago Bears.

Peripheral Vision

One of a defensive lineman's greatest assets is often his level of peripheral vision. The ability to see the peripheral action enables the defensive lineman to respond to the blocking scheme's development, as well as avoid injury. A defensive lineman must constantly be alert for a blocker coming at him from an unexpected direction. Intensive film study of an opponent's individual habits and team blocking schemes allows the defensive player to develop a "mode of recognition" for dangerous situations that might occur—situations where he could be trapped or double-team blocked.

Toughness and Stamina

As a defensive line coach, you will consistently insert words and phrases into your teaching that refer to the need to develop and maintain a foundation of physical and mental strength—phrases such as "mental toughness," "tenacity," "determination," and "the right stuff." No position on a football team involves more violence than the defensive line. Regardless of whether a defensive lineman is successful on a play, he will face contact on every snap from scrimmage. It is rare, indeed, for a defensive lineman to make a hit on the ballcarrier without first having to physically whip an offensive lineman who possesses an above-average level of strength and, in some cases, an equally impressive amount of quickness off the ball.

A defensive lineman has to go 100 percent on every play or face humiliation and/or physical domination. More often than not, he has to defeat an opponent who is larger in stature, taller, and stronger (upper body–wise). Consequently, the defensive lineman must—in addition to being the physically quicker and faster player—be the physically tougher player. He has to learn to use the conditioning factor as his ally and wear down the bulkier offensive lineman over the course of the game. A smart defensive lineman knows that the conditioning factor is always in his favor. He also uses his skills of quickness to frustrate and befuddle the opponent's technique. Finally, on occasion, he must break all the rules of the "coaching points" and just do what it takes to make the play.

2

Stance, Alignment, and Assignment

To maximize his level of effectiveness on the gridiron, a football player must adhere to the three fundamental governing guidelines of play for his particular position—stance, alignment, and assignment. These guidelines remain relevant for each position, regardless of whether the player is a quarterback or a nose tackle.

Stance

Stance refers to the "ready" position, which the player assumes prior to the snap of the football. Coaching this aspect tends to be influenced by one of two general philosophies regarding the stance. One line of coaching thought places considerable emphasis on the stance, with some coaches even calling it the single most important factor that determines how well the player will execute his assignment. These coaches believe that effective defensive line play begins with a good stance—and, to an extent, this belief is shared by coaches of all sports and all philosophies.

The primary point on which the two coaching philosophies differ is the interpretation of the relative importance of the mechanical considerations of the presnap stance. Mechanical considerations (e.g., which foot is back, which hand is down) are typically major points of concern to those coaches who believe in the singular importance of rigid stance requirements. The counter argument to those who ascribe to a philosophy of the preeminent nature of the stance (an argument that is advanced by those coaches who have adopted a more liberal viewpoint of the essential features regarding the stance) is that it is the *comfort* of the stance that should be the crucial point of emphasis.

When deciding which philosophy you should adopt regarding the stance, you should keep in mind that it is critical that a player's stance facilitates his ability to move efficiently. Not only should it allow him to move expeditiously, but also explosively. Accordingly, a logical argument can be advanced that the mechanics of a defensive lineman's stance are not nearly as important as his ability to move from his stance. It follows that, as a defensive line coach, you should not "overcoach" the stance at the expense of the player's natural ability. In other words, coaching points involving the stance, such as which foot is up (i.e., staggered forward) or which hand is down, should not be allowed to interfere with the efforts to have a defensive lineman anchor the line of scrimmage and pursue to the ballcarrier.

The general rule of thumb when coaching the stance to defensive linemen is relatively straightforward: The younger and more inexperienced the athlete, the more attention you should give to coaching the stance. In turn, experienced, higher-level players (especially professional athletes who demonstrate exceptional skill at their positions) should not be "overcoached" on the parameters of a "good" stance.

The parameters of a proper stance are somewhat dependent upon the philosophy of the defensive scheme in which the defender is employed. If it is an attack scheme that calls for the defensive lineman to attack on the snap of the ball and read on the run, the defensive lineman should demonstrate a stance that has the following characteristics:
- Feet closely set with a sprinter's stagger. The player bunches up (i.e., aligns his back foot as close as possible to his front foot), so that he gains ground across the line of scrimmage on the first step.
- Buttocks high in the air with his nose tilted downward
- Eyes looking up at the screws of the offensive lineman's headgear, with the ball kept in his peripheral vision
- The up-hand placed on his up-knee so that he can push downward with his hand on takeoff
- A hair trigger (i.e., extreme sensitivity of his senses prior to the snap)

On the other hand, if the scheme is a read scheme that calls for the defensive lineman to first read the blocker's action and then react to the scheme, the defensive lineman should employ a stance that adheres to the following features:
- Feet set shoulder-width apart with a slight toe-to-heel stagger
- Buttocks level with his back, with his weight shifted onto his hips

- Eyes intensely focused on the screws of the offensive lineman's headgear
- The up-hand open and typically hanging loose, with his up-arm slightly flexed outside of his up-knee
- A slow trigger. Although he should be hypersensitive to his opponent's movement when compared to the hair trigger of the attack scheme, a reading defensive lineman should operate with a slower, more controlled trigger.

An important point to remember is that, regardless of whether he is playing an attack philosophy or a read philosophy, a defensive lineman often assumes a stance that is tailored to the demands set forth by the special circumstances he finds himself in at a particular moment in the game. For example, many read-scheme defensive linemen are directed to assume an attack stance in passing situations. By the same token, both attack-scheme and read-scheme defensive linemen will shift their weight forward to their hands or backward to their hips, depending upon the down-and-distance situation or the time factor in the game. In a similar vein, both attack-scheme and read-scheme defensive linemen will drop their center of gravity and get into a four-point stance when playing in goal-line and short-yardage situations.

The following factors are among the ways that a four-point stance is inherently different from a basic three-point stance:
- A four-point stance is more compact; the player's hands are closer to his toes.
- His elbows are bent and slightly pronated (i.e., turned outward) to help him get lower.
- His hips and buttocks are positioned at a much higher plane than normal.
- His neck is bowed, but his body is tilted downward so that he cannot see much more than the feet of the offensive linemen and the movement of the ball.

A player may tailor his stance to allow him to gain an edge from a specific position. For example, the defensive lineman who is aligned at the nose tackle position uses a more compact stance than a defender aligned at the defensive end position. A nose tackle faces a triple threat on every snap (i.e., the possibility of being blocked from head-on, from one side, or from both sides). In addition to encountering double-team and occasionally triple-team blocks, a nose tackle has to be able to play zone blocks, as well as angle blocks from either side. Consequently, a nose tackle should use a stance that enables him to attack a blocker coming from either side, as well as from directly in front of him.

Defensive ends may use an elongated stance with a slight point to the inside. By cocking his body to the inside, a defensive end shortens the corner, thereby giving himself a more direct path to the quarterback. Defensive ends may also point straight upfield in their stance. When pointing straight ahead (somewhat as a nose tackle might), a defensive end should keep his outside foot staggered behind the inside foot, which enables him to immediately gain width by stepping to the outside with his back foot upon recognition of pass. The outside-foot-back stagger also gives the defensive end an advantage against the threat of a double-team sealing him to the inside. He can use his outside foot to gain more leverage as he defeats the block of the lead blocker (i.e., the blocker from the outside of a double-team).

As a general rule, the closer to the ball that the defensive lineman aligns, the less pronounced the stagger of his feet should be. For example, a nose tackle should keep his feet on an even plane, while a wide defensive end should use a heel-to-toe stagger. All factors considered, defensive linemen should not normally position their feet in a stagger that is greater than heel-to-toe.

In some instances, however, defensive linemen can adjust the normal positioning of their feet. For example, a defensive end may slightly elongate his stance when the offense is in an obvious passing situation. Furthermore, whenever a defensive lineman's primary responsibility is linked to gaining a vertical push, he may elongate his stance and increase the stagger of his feet. Defensive linemen who are playing in the gap between two offensive linemen may also stretch out in a longer stance. The point to be emphasized, however, is that anytime that a defensive lineman exaggerates the stagger of his feet, he should keep his feet closer together. In this regard, the general rule is as follows: The greater the stagger, the less distance the feet should be set apart.

Another factor to consider regarding a defender's stance is whether a defensive lineman is to play on the defensive right or the defensive left. Traditionally, a defensive lineman who lines up to the right of the football will put his left hand down and his left foot back, while a defensive lineman who takes a position to the left of the football will put his right hand down and his right foot back. If you adhere to this philosophy of defensive line coaching, you should attempt to position your defensive linemen to the side of the ball that is opposite their dominant hand. In other words, a right-handed athlete should be assigned to play on the defensive left, while a left-handed athlete should be assigned to play on the defensive right. You should keep in mind that depending upon the circumstances, it may be entirely appropriate for you (as was discussed early in the chapter) to instruct a defensive lineman to play his position with his outside hand down and his outside foot back. In these instances, your coaching efforts should involve a particular emphasis on the proper footwork techniques.

One final point involving the stance is the importance of the fact that the stance of the player is the starting point of the defensive assignment. A stance must be such that it helps a player meet his objective after the snap. Accordingly, as a coach, you should tend to look favorably on a player's stance as long as it doesn't result in a waste of movement (e.g., false step, hitch step). Keep in mind that a technical flaw in a player's stance shouldn't necessarily be corrected in all instances. In that regard, the primary factor against which a stance should be held accountable is the criteria of success. If a player is operating from what his coach perceives to be a mechanically imperfect stance, and the player is highly effective, in theory that mechanically imperfect stance is, in fact, empirically flawless.

Nevertheless, under normal circumstances, the ideal defensive lineman's stance reflects several characteristics, including the following:
- The defender's weight is centered on the hips.
- His back is flat.
- His neck is bowed.
- His knee is in line with the corresponding toe (i.e., the right knee is in line with the right toe and the left knee is in line with the left toe).
- His off-hand is positioned so that it can quickly be punched into the blocker.

Alignment

Alignment refers to the specific location of a defender within the confines of the defensive line with regard to a particular offensive landmark. Accurately specifying where a defender should line up enables the defensive coach to designate which gap the defender is expected to control. Gap control involves a defender getting his head in the proper gap and achieving an appropriate level of penetration so that he can secure the necessary leverage on the blocker. Among the offensive landmarks that are commonly employed are the following:
- The A gap (i.e., the gap between the center and the guard)—The A gap is further delineated according to whether it's on the strongside (i.e., +A) or the weakside (i.e., –A) of the offensive formation.
- The B gap (i.e., the gap between the guard and the tackle)—The B gap is further delineated according to whether it's on the strongside (i.e., +B) or the weakside (i.e., –B) of the offensive formation.
- The C gap (i.e., the gap between the tackle and the tight end)—The C gap is further delineated according to whether it's on the strongside (i.e., +C) or the weakside (i.e., –C) of the offensive formation.
- The D gap (i.e., the area extending from outside of the tight end to the sideline)—The D gap is further delineated according to whether it's on the strongside (i.e., +D) or the weakside (i.e., –D) of the offensive formation.

In general, the four gaps are specified in the same manner on each side of the ball. On occasion, gaps are numbered instead of lettered (i.e., 1 gap, 2 gap, 3 gap, 4 gap). A few coaches label the gaps consecutively from right to left or from left to right. Despite the substantial number of innovative defensive coaches in the game, the generic identification of gaps by consecutively lettering A to D on each side of the ball is still the most common terminology used in coaching the defensive line (Diagram 2-1).

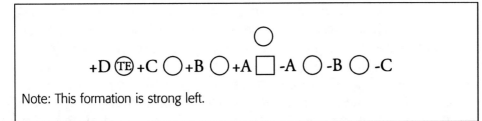

Note: This formation is strong left.

Diagram 2-1. Labeling gaps alphabetically

Another popular way of handling defensive line terminology involves giving defensive coaches a common ground to discuss the various details of defensive line play. This approach is designed to provide a basis to clearly identify the position of a defensive lineman along the line of scrimmage. In this concept of alignment terminology, the defensive lineman plays a numbered technique. Each numbered technique identifies a specific alignment over a particular offensive lineman. As illustrated in Diagram 2-2, the possible alignments are assigned a number. Each numerical technique corresponds to one of the following alignments:

- Head-up on the blocker
- Shaded to the inside of a blocker
- Shaded to the outside of a blocker
- In the gap between two blockers

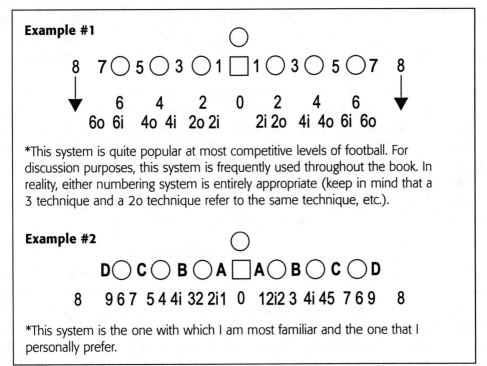

Diagram 2-2. Two examples of a generic alignment numbering system

In the first generic alignment numbering system illustrated in Diagram 2-2, an even-numbered technique corresponds to a head-up technique. Inside and outside shades are designated by assigning either an "i" (for inside) or an "o" (for outside). The second example of a generic alignment numbering system shown in Diagram 2-2 is similar to the first example. This approach also adheres to a system in which an even-numbered technique corresponds to a head-up technique. In this system (the classical defensive-line-technique numbering system that was developed by Bum Phillips), outside shades are odd-numbered techniques. The 7 technique is the one exception to this rule. In this system, the 7 technique is the only inside shade technique identified by an odd number. The remaining inside shades are specified by even numbers accompanied by the letter "i."

To differentiate between a head-up technique and an inside shade technique, the letter "i" is used to specify when the even-numbered technique is an inside shade—and not a head-up alignment. For example, the inside shade alignment on the offensive guard is called a 2i technique, while an outside shade alignment on the offensive tackle is called a 4i technique.

Another problematic aspect of the classical (generic) numbering system occurs when you attempt to identify a gap technique. With one exception, no identifying number for a gap alignment exists in the classical system. Therefore, to identify the particular gap in which the defender is to align, you should either assign the gap a letter designation or add the word "gap" after the technique number. For example, in the latter option, when a defender aligns in the gap between the guard and tackle, he aligns in a 4 gap. You could also accurately describe that particular gap alignment as a 3 gap. The designation of a defender aligned in the guard-tackle gap as either a 4 gap or a 3 gap is a matter of preference and a matter of what name fits best within your system. In a similar vein, a defender who aligns in the gap between the tackle and the tight end may be designated by one of two names. In the classical number system, the defender aligned in the tackle–tight end gap may be accurately named a 5 gap or a 7 gap. Again, the choice of which term is best is one of personal preference. Somewhat ironically, the classical numbering system provides a name for the defender who is aligned in the center-guard gap (the only gap alignment number in the entire classical numbering system). This defender is called a 1 technique.

Due to the inherent problems (i.e., inconsistencies) in the classical (generic) technique numbering system, several alternative numbering concepts have been developed and put into coaching practice. For example, several of the numbering concepts currently in use eliminate the inconsistency of the system regarding where the technique is numbered over the tight end position. In this regard, the most common revision of the classical (generic) numbering of the techniques over the tight end results in a more consistent theme within the numbering concept. As illustrated in Diagram 2-3, this particular approach to numbering assigns the inside alignment on each offensive player an even number. For example, the inside shade on the offensive guard remains a 2i technique, while the inside shade on the offensive tackle remains a 4i technique. The inside shade on the tight end, however, is assigned the number 6i, instead of the number 7.

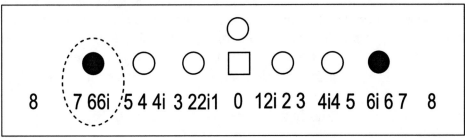

Diagram 2-3. The classical (generic) numbering system revision at the defensive end position

Detailed Alignment Specifications

Every technique numbering system is structured to include the three basic alignments—inside, head up, and outside. The two shade alignments are the inside and outside alignments. In most numbering systems, a player is shaded when he aligns to one side of the blocker. If the defensive player aligns inside (i.e., between the ball and the blocker), the defender is playing an inside shade. On the other hand, if the defender aligns outside (i.e., the defender is positioned so that the blocker is between him and the ball), the defender is playing an outside shade. Inside shades have been traditionally referred to as "inside-eye" alignments, while outside shades have been called "outside-eye" alignments.

The origination of the "eye" terminology comes from the approach that the defensive player should match one of his eyes to one of the blocker's eyes. For example, a 5-technique tackle plays an outside-eye alignment. Therefore, the defensive player who is playing the 5-technique position aligns so that his inside eye is directly in front of the offensive tackle's outside eye. As you might imagine, a wide range of discrepancy is possible with regard to individual interpretations of exactly what is an inside-eye or outside-eye alignment. Not surprisingly, it is easy to conclude that a player's eyeball is not a particularly good reference point for alignment.

A much more acceptable method for accurately aligning defensive linemen in a consistent shade involves having the defender position his foot on a plane cutting through the blocker's stance. Three such planes exist. One plane splits the stance into two even parts. Called the midline plane, this plane splits the crotch of the blocker. The second plane—called the inside plane—runs parallel to the instep of the blocker's inside foot. The third plane—christened the outside plane—runs parallel to the instep of the blocker's outside foot. Diagram 2-4 shows the stance of an offensive player and the three dissecting planes of the blocker's stance.

To realize the full advantage of identifying the three planes that cut through the offensive lineman's stance, the defender must specify one of his feet as his "leverage foot," while designating the other foot as his "anchor foot." Given the fact that the defender must keep "leverage" in his gap, the leverage foot is the foot that he must keep free in his gap responsibility. Consequently, the defender's gapside foot is his leverage foot. Conversely, the defender's opposite foot is his anchor foot. Proper positioning of the anchor foot guarantees that the defensive lineman will align in the precise location desired—as a shade, a crotch, or a shadow technique.

- The 2i, 2, 4i, 4, and 7 techniques use the foot furthest from the ball as the anchor foot.

- The 0, 3, 5, and 9 techniques use the foot closest to the ball as the anchor foot.

- The 1 technique aligns in the A gap and has no designated anchor foot.

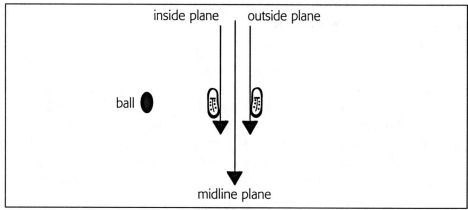

Diagram 2-4. The three planes of a defender that intersect the offensive lineman's stance

Outside Techniques (3, 5, and 9 Techniques)

When a defensive lineman assumes his stance, he places his anchor foot on one of the three intersecting planes of the offensive lineman's stance. The outside defender (i.e., the 3 technique, the 5 technique, or the 9 technique) uses his inside foot as his anchor foot. If an outside technique places his anchor foot on the inside plane of the blocker's stance, he is aligning in a shade alignment (Diagram 2-5). The shade alignment is the tightest alignment variation of any numbered technique. A tight alignment is an alignment that is as close as possible to head-up on the blocker, without actually being head up. For example, a 3-technique defender aligns on the guard and has B-gap responsibility. Like all outside techniques, his anchor foot is his foot closest to the ball. The 3 technique's leverage foot is the foot closest to the B gap. By placing his anchor foot on the inside plane, the 3 technique aligns in the tightest possible 3-technique alignment (the shade 3-technique alignment). On the other hand, if a 3-technique defender were to place his foot directly in front of the guard's inside foot, his alignment would no longer fall under the definition of a 3 technique. At that point, he would then be a 2 technique (refer to Diagram 2-2).

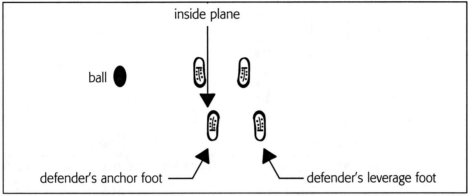

Diagram 2-5. The shade alignment of the outside technique (e.g., the 3, 5, and 9 techniques)

When an outside technique places his anchor foot on the midline plane, his anchor foot points directly at the offensive lineman's crotch. Accordingly, this alignment is called a crotch alignment (Diagram 2-6). The crotch alignment is typically used for any odd-numbered technique. Likewise, the usual alignment for the even-numbered "i" techniques (e.g., 2i and 4i techniques) is also the crotch alignment.

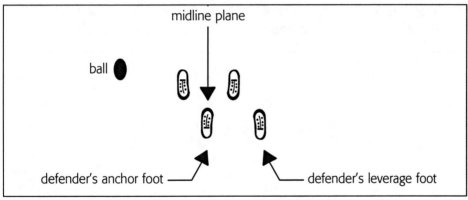

Diagram 2-6. The crotch alignment of the outside defender (e.g., the 3, 5, and 9 techniques)

When an outside technique places his anchor foot on the outside plane, he aligns in a shadow alignment (Diagram 2-7). A shadow alignment is also known as a "loose" alignment. In a shadow alignment, the outside-technique lineman plays from his widest alignment. Should the defensive lineman move out wider than an outside technique, the defensive tackle's alignment would be classified as a gap-technique alignment. The shadow alignment is a good adjustment for the outside technique to assume versus foot-to-foot (i.e., very tight) offensive line splits, and also in pass-rushing situations, regardless of the offensive line splits.

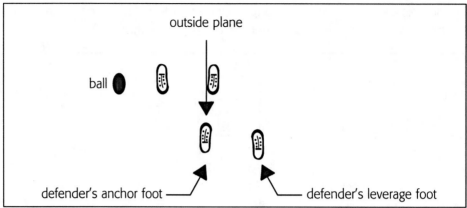

Diagram 2-7. The shadow alignment of an outside technique (e.g., the 3, 5, and 9 techniques)

Inside Techniques (2, 4, and 7 Techniques)

The inside-technique defender uses his outside foot as his anchor foot. If an inside-technique defender places his anchor foot on the outside plane of the blocker's stance, he is in a shade alignment (Diagram 2-8). For example, a 2i-technique defender assumes a shade 2i alignment when he places his outside foot on the outside plane of the guard's stance. Likewise, a 4i-technique defender takes on a shade 4i alignment when he places his outside foot on the outside plane of the tackle's stance. Similarly, a 7-technique defender is positioned in a shade 7-technique alignment when he places his outside foot on the outside plane of the tight end's stance.

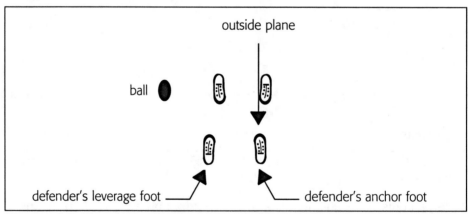

Diagram 2-8. The shade alignment of an inside technique (e.g., the 2, 4, and 7 techniques)

When an inside technique places his anchor foot on the midline plane, his anchor foot points directly at the offensive lineman's crotch. This alignment is the crotch alignment of the inside technique (Diagram 2-9). Remember, the crotch alignment is the standard alignment of the inside techniques.

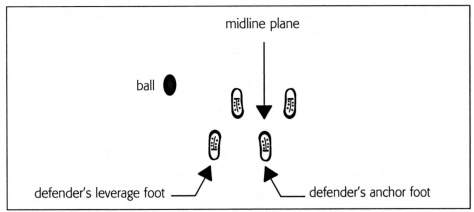

Diagram 2-9. The crotch alignment of an inside technique (e.g., the 2, 4, and 7 techniques)

The shadow alignment (Diagram 2-10) of an inside-technique defender is the tightest available alignment to the ball. For example, a shadow 4i defender is closer to the B gap than he is to the offensive tackle. The inside-technique defender aligns in a shadow alignment when he feels that the gap closest to his leverage foot is too wide for the offensive lineman to control. The shadow alignment allows the inside-technique defender to beat the blocker by blitzing through the gap. The shadow alignment should never be used when the offensive line splits are relatively narrow.

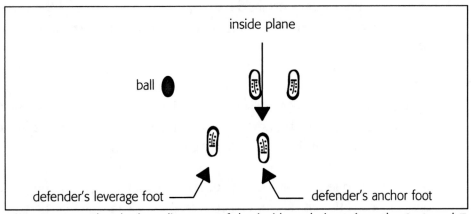

Diagram 2-10. The shadow alignment of the inside technique (e.g., the 2, 4, and 7 techniques)

0 Technique Shade and Shadow

The head-up 0-technique nose tackle doesn't have the luxury of an "inside" or "outside" reference foot. However, if a nose tackle assumes a shade alignment or a crotch alignment, he must offset his alignment to one side of the ball. Once the nose tackle offsets to one side, he then establishes an "inside" foot and an "outside" foot. The offset nose tackle's inside foot is his anchor foot, while his outside foot is his leverage foot. The center's inside plane naturally corresponds to the inside anchor foot of the offset nose tackle. These facts established, the shade 0 technique aligns with his inside foot on the outside plane of the center. Table 2-1 provides an overview of the foot positioning points for the three basic types of alignments (shade, crotch, and shadow) for both outside and inside techniques.

Outside Techniques:
- A shade 0 technique puts his inside foot on the inside of the center.
- A shade 3 technique puts his inside foot on the inside plane of the guard.
- A shade 5 technique puts his inside foot on the inside plane of the tackle.
- A shade 9 technique puts his inside foot on the inside plane of the tight end or third man.
- A crotch 0 technique puts his inside foot on the midline plane of the center.
- A crotch 3 technique puts his inside foot on the midline plane of the guard.
- A crotch 5 technique puts his inside foot on the midline plane of the tackle.
- A crotch 9 technique puts his inside foot on the midline plane of the tight end or the third man.
- A shadow 0 technique puts his inside foot on the outside plane of the center.
- A shadow 3 technique puts his inside foot on the outside plane of the guard.
- A shadow 5 technique puts his inside foot on the outside plane of the tackle.
- A shadow 9 technique puts his inside foot on the outside plane of the tight end or the third man.

Inside Techniques:
- A shade 2i technique puts his outside foot on the outside plane of the guard.
- A shade 4i technique puts his outside foot on the outside plane of the tackle.
- A shade 7 technique puts his outside foot on the outside plane of the tight end or the third man.
- A crotch 2i technique puts his outside foot on the midline plane of the guard.
- A crotch 4i technique puts his outside foot on the midline plane of the tackle.
- A crotch 7 technique puts his outside foot on the midline plane of the tight end or the third man.
- A shadow 2i technique puts his outside foot on the inside plane of the guard.
- A shadow 4i technique puts his outside foot on the inside plane of the tackle.
- A shadow 7 technique puts his outside foot on the inside plane of the tight end or the third man.

Table 2-1. Foot positioning points for the shade, crotch, and shadow alignments

Assignment

Two main types of positions exist on the defensive line—tackle and end. The position that a lineman plays is usually compatible with his size, strength, height, weight, and speed. Defensive tackles are typically stronger and heavier than defensive ends. A taller athlete who possesses a relatively higher level of speed is normally assigned to play the defensive end position. Agility is a characteristic that is required of both positions. All factors considered, it is unlikely that a player who doesn't have an above-average level of agility for his size will be successful at either defensive line position.

Two basic philosophies exist in football regarding the configuration of the defensive line—the seven-man front and the eight-man front. The modern eight-man front is characterized by a front of two tackles and two defensive ends. Of the seven-man fronts, two types of alignments are standard—the odd seven-man front and the even seven-man front. The even seven-man front is similar in nature to the eight-man front. Like the eight-man front, the even seven-man front is composed of two tackles and two ends. The odd seven-man front is the only front that includes a nose tackle. In effect, the nose tackle of the odd front gives the scheme the unique feature of having three defensive tackles. Table 2-2 provides a list of the most commonly employed eight-man and seven-man fronts, along with their defensive line makeup.

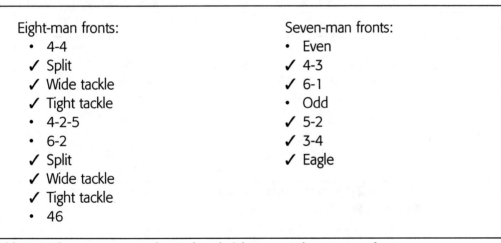

Eight-man fronts:	Seven-man fronts:
• 4-4	• Even
✓ Split	✓ 4-3
✓ Wide tackle	✓ 6-1
✓ Tight tackle	• Odd
• 4-2-5	✓ 5-2
• 6-2	✓ 3-4
✓ Split	✓ Eagle
✓ Wide tackle	
✓ Tight tackle	
• 46	

Table 2-2. The most commonly employed eight-man and seven-man fronts

Diagrams of Common Eight-Man Fronts

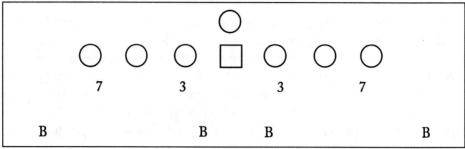

Diagram 2-11. The 4-4 split front according to the classical (generic) numbering system

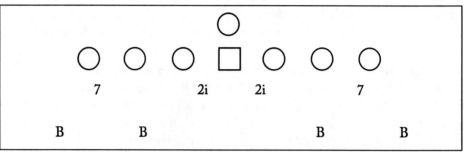

Diagram 2-12. The 4-4 wide tackle front according to the classical (generic) numbering system

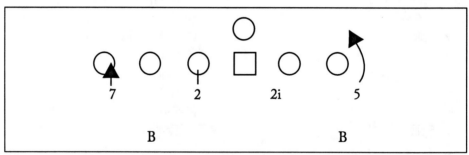

Diagram 2-13. The 4-2-5 front (i.e., overslide to the tight end) according to the classical (generic) numbering system

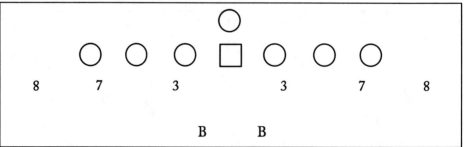

Diagram 2-14. The 6-2 split front according to the classical (generic) numbering system

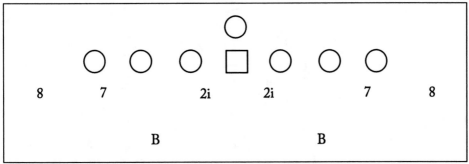

Diagram 2-15. The 6-2 wide tackle front according to the classical (generic) numbering system

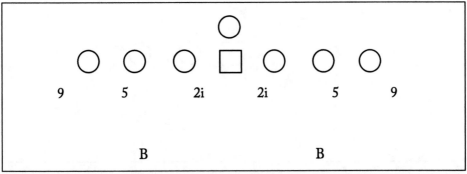

Diagram 2-16. The 6-2 tight tackle front according to the classical (generic) numbering system

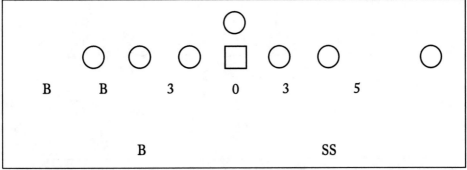

Diagram 2-17. The 46 front according to the classical (generic) numbering system

Diagrams of Common Seven-Man Fronts

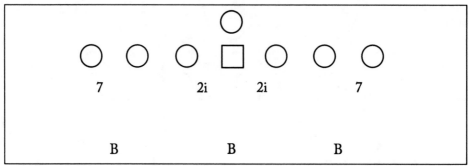

Diagram 2-18. The 4-3 front according to the classical (generic) numbering system

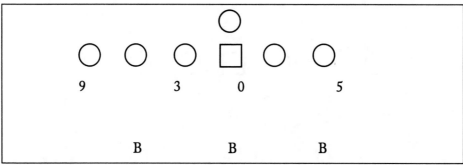

Diagram 2-19. The Miami 4-3 front according to the classical (generic) numbering system

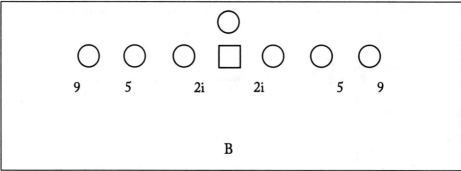

Diagram 2-20. The 6-1 front according to the classical (generic) numbering system

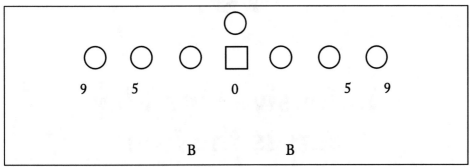

Diagram 2-21. The 5-2 front according to the classical (generic) numbering system

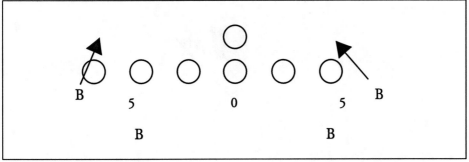

Diagram 2-22. The 3-4 front according to the classical (generic) numbering system

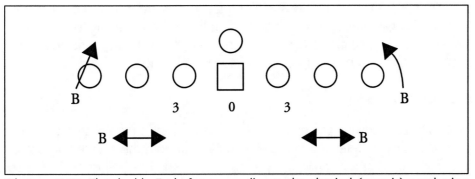

Diagram 2-23. The double Eagle front according to the classical (generic) numbering system

3

Defensive Line Play
Versus the Run

Philosophy

The most important rule of defensive line play versus the run is that a lineman can never leave his gap until he can guarantee that the ball is not going to be run there in all run defenses. Beyond this basic requirement, a team's philosophy of defensive line play against the run is dependent upon the personal preferences of the defensive coach.

The Attack Philosophy

Several significant advantages exist for a defensive lineman in an attack scheme. An attack philosophy of defensive line play is utilized in both the seven- and eight-man-front schemes. An attack philosophy (i.e., read-on-the-run philosophy) has several distinct advantages over a read philosophy (i.e., read-then-run philosophy). Among the perceived advantages of an attack technique over a read technique are the following:

- An attack technique forces the offensive linemen to defend against penetration. One likely result of such a scenario is tentative play along the offensive line, as each offensive lineman tends to be overly concerned about "stopping" the defender's penetration instead of focusing on "firing off" on the defender. To a point, any time an offensive lineman unduly focuses on such steps as "defending" or "stopping," that offensive lineman is essentially "defeated."

- An attack technique forces the offensive line coach to double-team at the point of attack. Keep in mind that, as a rule, a hard-charging defensive lineman can only be neutralized by a similarly hard-charging offensive lineman. To an offensive line coach, neutralization is better than penetration, because neutralization implies that a stalemate has occurred. Instead, an offensive line coach should view a stalemate as a situation that is synonymous with failure. The point to remember is that under most circumstances, the offensive line must create a new line of scrimmage, gain a push along the front, and use their leverage to create seams for the running back. A stalemated offensive lineman can accomplish none of these objectives. Consequently, the most basic strategy in gaining an offensive edge at the point of attack versus an attack-style defensive lineman is the double-team strategy, but the defense gains a numerical advantage in its pursuit when the double-team is forced at the point of attack.
- An attack technique tends to destroy the integrity of the offensive line's schematics. Versus an attacking defensive line, the offensive line coach must design his game plan in deference to his opponent's defensive philosophy. Offensive considerations, such as line splits (i.e., the distance between the linemen), alignment depth (i.e., the blocker's distance from the line of scrimmage), individual blocking technique, and even play selection, must be carefully evaluated prior to the game to see if these factors should be adjusted. If they must, to what degree should they be adjusted? An entirely new dimension is added to a team's offensive preparation efforts when its opponent's defensive philosophy is based from an attack scheme on the defensive line.
- An attack technique frees the defensive line to wreak havoc and disrupt the continuity of the blocking scheme. All factors considered, by charging upfield on the snap, a defensive lineman becomes the "hunter." As most defensive coaches agree, movement is one of the keys to success on the offensive line. If such a consensus is, in fact, correct, then movement should be the presnap objective of the defensive lineman. Each defensive lineman should remember to gear his reactions to a hair-trigger level of sensitivity and to attack to get his head in the gap. This approach forces the offensive lineman to adjust to the defender's attacking technique. As a rule, in trench play, the player who forces his opponent to make an adjustment has the advantage. Not surprisingly, the player who is forced to adjust is at a significant advantage. It follows that the defensive lineman who attacks the line of scrimmage on the snap of the ball gains a measure of "instant superiority." In doing so, such a lineman obtains the persona of a linebacker—"a hunter."
- An attack technique maximizes the talent and the skills of every athlete. In some instances, an attack scheme can even enable an undersized defensive lineman to dominate the line of scrimmage. All factors considered, a defensive lineman playing within an attack scheme can get more done with relatively less physical skill. He can overcome mismatches of strength, quickness, and size—all because of

the jump he gets by keying the ball and attacking a specific area or gap, rather than waiting for the movement of a particular offensive lineman to cue him to anchor and control the blocker.

- Waiting to read the blocking scheme and slide horizontally upon establishing control of the blocker is a skill that few athletes can physically accomplish. On the other hand, attacking to establish a new line of scrimmage and wreak havoc on the offensive scheme is a skill that most athletes can accomplish. As a rule, the stronger, more talented athlete who is capable of playing well within a read philosophy will be even more effective in the attack philosophy.

- While an attack technique may limit the ability of some defenders to physically focus on the peripheral action, well-trained, hard-charging defensive linemen tend to be acutely aware of the peripheral problems. Knowledge of this situation and proper and constant practice in the recognition of, and reaction to, these dangers can enable an attack-scheme defensive lineman to develop a finely honed skill in reacting to peripheral threats, such as traps and angle blocks.

- An attack style of defense is designed to let a defensive lineman play. He doesn't need a defensive call to inform him that he should gear up and rush the passer. He is geared up on every play. He doesn't require a defensive call to tell him to attack instead of read; he attacks on every snap of the ball. An attack style puts the game into the hands of the athlete. All factors considered, it removes "thinking" from the defender's action equation. In the process, the defender is given the opportunity to concentrate on the physical dimension of trench play.

The Read Philosophy

For the sake of presenting a balanced review of the subject of an attack versus a read philosophy of defensive play (particularly for those defensive line coaches who feel more comfortable with a read philosophy of defensive line play), it is important to keep in mind that a few coaching points exist that support the merits of a read philosophy over an attack philosophy. Because the read philosophy is based upon some excellent coaching points, it is not surprising that this philosophy is used by coaches at the higher competitive levels of play.

- The read scheme gives a defensive lineman a greater degree of leverage in horizontal control. An attack philosophy, on the other hand, can create seams in the front as the defensive linemen charge upfield on the snap.

- The read scheme provides a defensive lineman with an increased level of pursuit to the ballcarrier, whereas an attack philosophy causes the defender to change his pursuit angle if the ball does not immediately hit in his area.

- The read scheme frees the linebackers. An attack philosophy, on the other hand, puts more pressure on the linebackers to stop the interior traps and hard dives and requires them to fill their gap assignments immediately.

- The read scheme provides an opportunity for the defensive lineman to maximize the impact of his personal level of strength and, in the process, control the opposing blocker. To a point, an attack philosophy—because of its emphasis on the defender's vertical push—may compromise the potential effect that a defensive lineman's level of strength actually has on a play.
- The read scheme allows the defensive lineman to use his peripheral vision. On the other hand, an attack scheme may have a negative impact on the effect of a defender's peripheral vision, because the defensive lineman's ability to react to peripheral threats is compromised to a degree by his vertical charge on the snap.

Control Schemes

One-Gap Control

In both the eight- and seven-man-front schemes, an attack philosophy is conducive to "one-gap" control. One-gap control is an important concept in coaching defensive line play. A lineman who is playing in a one-gap control scheme is afforded the freedom of vertical penetration. This feature refers to the fact that a one-gap control player can possess and utilize his hair-trigger reactions and be assigned (as desired) the task of attacking the line of scrimmage.

The freedom granted a defensive lineman in the one-gap system makes him a forceful threat to push a point and force a break in the continuity of the offensive line unit. "Pushing a point" is a phrase used to describe the action of a defensive lineman when he creates a bubble in the offensive line by charging straight ahead on the snap. If he breaks through the resistance, he has pushed a point through the line of scrimmage and forced a break in the continuity of the offensive line. The offensive line usually responds to situations in which vertical penetration has occurred by downgrading their priorities from knocking people off the ball and achieving movement to assuming a more passive stance.

The passive stance is a by-product of the mental state of an offensive lineman who becomes acutely aware of defensive penetration. In the passive stance, an offensive lineman quickly begins to guard against penetration and focus on "damage control." Collectively, the offensive line simply hopes to maintain the offensive integrity at the line of scrimmage. Once a passive stance is established within the offensive line, an argument can be advanced that the game within the game—in the trenches—belongs to the defense at that point.

Not only is one-gap control a popular style of play at both the collegiate and interscholastic levels of play, it is also the predominant style of defensive line play in the National Football League. Because of its advantages, it appears that the one-gap control philosophy of defensive line play is appropriate for athletes at all competitive levels (from young inexperienced players to pro athletes). Among the perceived benefits of one-gap control are the following:

- It allows the defensive lineman to use a dominant shoulder in his technique.
- It enables the defensive lineman to attack on the snap and read on the run.
- It permits the defensive lineman to threaten the offensive line with a vertical push.
- It provides an opportunity for the defensive lineman to get a jump into his pass-rush move much more quickly upon pass recognition.

Two-Gap Control

The read technique is the only suitable style of play for the two-gap philosophy of defensive line play. The two-gap control player, as the phrase implies, is responsible for the control and anchoring of two gaps instead of just one. This assignment is a pure two-gap assignment only in the moments before the ball is snapped. Once the ball is snapped and the point of attack is recognized, the two-gap player becomes a one-gap player. The defender makes such a transformation by correctly reading the blocking scheme or blocking key.

If the defender's key shows the ball moving toward one of the two gaps for which he is responsible, that defender immediately becomes a one-gap player in the direction of the key's movement, forsaking the opposite gap. Thus, a two-gap lineman plays under the guidelines of the art of "reading the hat." A two-gap control player reads the hat (i.e., the headgear of the blocker) when he reacts to the offensive player moving his head in one direction. When reading the hat, the defensive player's objective is to gain leverage in the gap ahead of the blocker's movement. In other words, if a two-gap nose tackle reads the center's headgear moving to the nose tackle's right shoulder, he attempts to get his left shoulder across the headgear of the center, thereby beating the center across his face and gaining leverage in the playside gap. Not surprisingly, the two-gap technique can be effective when it is used by an extremely big and strong defensive lineman.

While theoretically a sound practice, the two-gap control philosophy of defensive line play is much more difficult to master on the field. In contrast, the one-gap control system of play can be easily taught by the coach and quickly mastered by the athlete at all levels of competitive play.

Unlike the two-gap philosophy, the one-gap control system enables the defensive player to dominate the line of scrimmage as he focuses on a single point on the opponent, instead of waiting to read the blocker. Most importantly, the one-gap control system allows the defensive lineman to attack the line of scrimmage on the snap of the football and read on the run. All factors considered, most defensive line coaches tend to favor a system that enables their players to attack on the snap and read the action on the run.

Defensive Line Techniques

Throwing–the-Hands Technique

If a rule was passed to limit the coaching instruction of defensive line play to a single word, an individual could still be an effective line coach—if the one word he chose to use was "hands." The hands are the primary key to successful line play. While the feet, legs, hips, and shoulders each have an essential role in effective defensive line play, these body parts are simply not as critical as the defender's hands. Although these components serve an integral function in performing defensive line techniques properly, their ultimate level of effectiveness hinges on the proper use of the throwing-the-hands technique.

The importance of the proper use of the defender's hands is more easily understood once the movement of an attacking lineman is broken down and analyzed. If the motion of the attacking defensive lineman is examined, it can be seen that the hands lead the body. The faster the hands are thrown into the opponent, the more momentum (and consequently the more force) he will generate. When the defender's hands are violently thrown into the body of the blocker, the defender's hips snap forward and his buttocks sink. The defender's powerful hamstrings flex as his knees instantly bend to concentrate the power in his lower body in his hamstrings, buttocks, and the balls of his feet.

Most coaches (particularly those working with relatively inexperienced players) have encountered the need for teaching their athletes to keep their heads back to avoid contacting an opponent with the head. Often, an inexperienced player will try to please his coach by fearlessly attacking an opponent. In the process, he tends to put his head down. This action can result in a serious injury to the athlete's head, neck, and spine. By emphasizing the need to properly execute the throwing-the-hands technique, even in youth leagues, the action of a defender putting his head down when making contact with a blocker can virtually be eliminated.

Throwing the hands forces the defender's head to recoil behind the plane of his shoulders. Although most young football players don't possess the upper-body strength to realize the full benefits of the throwing-the-hands technique, teaching this technique to such athletes does offer several potential advantages, including the fact that it has a positive impact on learning how to properly execute a shoulder-blow delivery—the more effective technique in youth play.

Regardless of the style or level of play, when a defensive lineman throws his hands, his forearms and shoulders naturally follow. As such, the throwing-the-hands technique can be easily modified for the shoulder-blow delivery technique. To modify the "hands" technique, the defender simply has to throw his hands so that the front of his hand faces the defender on contact. Rolling the hands in this manner forces the defender's elbow outward, so that his forearm and shoulder can be used as an attack surface.

Athletes at the more competitive levels of play should be trained to concentrate more on using their hands to gain separation from a blocker. To gain separation, a defender must first gain control through the proper placement of his hands. Hand placement involves two factors—"how" and "where." "How" refers to how the defender uses his hands when making contact with a blocker's body. "Where" refers to where on a blocker's body the defender places his hands.

The defensive lineman should be trained to use his hands in a manner that jolts the blocker. Ideally, a defensive lineman will use his hands to stun the blocker. A defensive lineman should instantaneously lift the blocker by using his upper-body strength and by locking out his arms. He should then bench press the blocker away from his body, feel the direction of the flow of the ball, execute a quick release off the blocker, and pursue the ballcarrier.

In reality, however, a defensive lineman will rarely, if ever, gain a full lockout position on an offensive blocker. For example, even the strongest linemen in the National Football League seldom can get to this position against an opponent of even average skill. Accordingly, the best that any defensive line coach can usually hope for is for his player to achieve a partial lockout and to release off the blocker. A partial lockout is accomplished when the defensive lineman gains separation from the blocker, but does not fully extend his arms (i.e., his arms remain bent).

Most coaches agree that gaining a straight-arm lockout on the blocker offers a greater factor of resistance. The opposite side of that coin is the fact that bent arms offer a greater factor of power. All factors considered, power is clearly a more desirable attribute than resistance. Power makes reference to the capacity to exert force, while resistance refers only to an opposition to force. Merely offering resistance is not enough; the defensive lineman should strike a blow (i.e., exert a force) against the blocker. In this regard, the straight-arm locked-out arm position that most defensive coaches want their athletes to obtain is not the ideal position. Scientific laws of leverage arms and simply machinery support the argument that bent arms indeed offer more potential for exerting power. As a result, the partial lockout position (ironically) becomes the ideal lockout position.

The potential for power not withstanding, the bench-press lockout technique should still be taught. In the process of teaching this ideal method, the defensive coach is likely to find that his defensive linemen will actually achieve adequate separation through a partial lockout.

Ideally, the defensive lineman should throw his hands so that he strikes his opponent's blocking surface with the heels of his hands. Much consideration has been given to the placement of the thumbs when the blow is struck. It appears that most coaches believe that the positioning of the thumbs should be left to personal preference.

Some coaches teach the "thumbs-up" method, in which the fingers are slightly flexed and loosely bent so that the defensive lineman can grab cloth. This type of hand positioning is called a "chuck" grasp—a dual reference to the clamp-like took and the quick-throwing motion of the same name. The defensive lineman uses his chuck grasp to control a blocker and feel the pressure, so that he may throw the blocker away from his angle of pursuit and sprint to the ballcarrier.

Some athletes prefer to roll their thumbs inward or downward on contact. The major negative factor involved in doing so is that such an action causes the defender's elbows to point outward. This position offers little power to the defensive lineman, since his elbows are out of line with his main thrust of force. To maximize his power, an experienced defensive lineman should keep his elbows inside the frame of his upper body, exactly as his elbows should be when he is bench pressing. This position enables a defensive lineman to increase his power by keeping the force moving in a direct line. A major coaching point to emphasize in this regard is that a defensive lineman should prevent his thumbs from rolling inward or downward on contact. Throwing the hands and striking a blow into the blocker with the thumbs pointing upward not only helps a defensive lineman to keep his elbows in, it also increases his power factor.

Where the hands are placed is primarily dependent upon the relative height of the blocking surface (i.e., the blocker's shoulders). If the blocker comes off the ball in a relatively high posture, the plane of the blocking surface is consequently high (possibly above the shoulders of the defensive lineman). If the blocker comes off the ball in a scrambling, ultra-low posture, the blocking surface is relatively low (probably well below the defensive lineman's knees). The defender's hands should be thrown to a common plane—the plane at which a blocker carries his shoulders when executing a normal base block. If the blocker comes off the ball with a high blocking surface above the common plane, the defensive lineman has a good shot at striking a forceful blow into the blocker's numbers and lifting the blocker's shoulders. On the other hand, if the blocker comes off the ball below the common plane to attack the knees of the defensive lineman, the defender can adjust the angle of his hands so that he strikes the blocker on his shoulder pads and drives his head downward into the playing surface.

It is important that a defender be coached to keep his eyes focused on the screws. He cannot afford to peer through a blocker's headgear to look for the ball. He should have a twofold primary objective—defeat the blocker and stay on his feet. Failing to maintain a focus on the screws often results in the defensive player getting cut down by a low blocker. Unrelenting focusing on the screws of the blocker is an essential factor in the defensive lineman being able to defeat a scramble blocker and stay on his feet.

Forearm-and-Shoulder Blow-Delivery Technique

The forearm and shoulder are not separate blow-delivery mechanisms. They are both part of a single technique. The forearm-and-shoulder blow is an excellent technique against any block. When a lineman is delivering a forearm-and-shoulder blow, the elbow is allowed to fly outward. Because the elbow points outward on contact, the thumb points upward, with the defender's palm facing him. The defensive lineman can also make a fist with his blow-delivery hand as he strikes the chest of the blocker with the front of his hand and the outside of his arm. The relatively compact physical characteristics of the forearm-and-shoulder blow increase the speed of the defender's arm and shoulder in striking the blocker.

The hand and the arm provide a lift to the blow delivery. When this technique is employed, the defender's shoulder should actually stop the charge of the blocker, stunning him in such a way that his forearm can provide the desired lift and separation. The procedure's name—the forearm-and-shoulder technique—is actually a misnomer. The technique should more accurately be described as the shoulder-and-forearm technique.

If aligned in a gap technique in a goal-line situation, the defensive lineman should use both shoulders to deliver the blow. He should penetrate the gap in a low charge, while delivering an uplifting force with each shoulder. This action prevents him from being knocked off course to one side and ensures that he can push a point through the line of scrimmage and destroy the continuity of the offensive scrimmage line. The gap charge is the only time that a defensive lineman should use both shoulders as blow-delivery mechanisms. Normally, a defensive lineman should execute a forearm-and-shoulder blow with the shoulder that is furthest from his responsible gap and closest to the man on which he is aligned. That is to say, if a defensive lineman aligned on the guard is responsible for the B gap, he should use his inside shoulder to attack the guard. Likewise, if the defensive lineman aligned on the tackle is responsible for the same B gap, he should use his outside shoulder to attack the tackle.

When a forearm-and-shoulder blow-delivery technique is executed from a shade alignment, the defensive lineman should visualize throwing his forearm—instead of his hands—into the blocker. No motion is wasted as the defender's forearm and fist lead his shoulder into the blocker's chest. The defensive lineman's off-hand immediately follows his active forearm in contacting the blocker. Defensive linemen should be taught to use their off-hand to strike the blocker in a manner that is similar to the throwing-the-hands technique.

The defensive lineman should use the heel of his hand to strike the blocker inside the plane of the blocker's upper body. Using the chuck grasp, the defensive lineman should grab cloth and do one of two things. The first option is to jerk the blocker's shoulder down. This action turns the blocker's shoulders and twists him so that he loses his blocking surface. The defensive lineman should then quickly release off the blocker and go to the football.

The second option is to jam and extend the chuck hand so that the blocker's shoulder twists backward. This action also causes the blocker to lose his square blocking surface. Jamming the blocker's shoulder backward enables the defensive lineman to bring his blow-delivery shoulder across the face of the blocker and clear the blocker. Through regular repetition in practice, the defensive lineman should develop a better feel for which option he needs to execute. Eventually, he should be able to make this decision instantaneously, and then use his off-hand to pull or push the blocker's shoulder and escape to tackle the ballcarrier.

Even when employing the more desirable throwing-the-hands technique, a defensive lineman may encounter an away block. Several types of away blocks exist, including zone blocks, scoop blocks, offside blocks, and angle blocks. Whenever an offensive lineman executes one of these blocks, the defensive lineman must convert his technique, while moving from a throwing-the-hands technique to a forearm-and-shoulder blow-delivery. When an offensive lineman blocks away, he loses some or all of his blocking surface. Since an offensive lineman turns his shoulders on an away block, little surface area is left for the defender's hands to contact. In this instance, a defensive lineman would have to turn his shoulders to be able to get his hands into the chest of the blocker.

Converting from a throwing-the-hands technique to delivering a shoulder blow enables a defensive lineman to keep his shoulders square and still deliver a forceful shoulder shiver into the backside shoulder of the away blocker. In other words, a defensive lineman can still get a piece of the blocker, even though the blocker is vacating the immediate area of the defender. Such a conversion also helps a defensive lineman to close toward an away block. Closing down to the blocker helps a defensive team to maintain integrity along the defensive front and gives the defensive lineman an opportunity to play the cutback, as well as drive off his inside leg and redirect to rush the bootleg.

A trapping offensive lineman often explodes into the vision of the defensive lineman. Figuratively, he appears like a "truck in the mist," barreling down on the defensive lineman's inside knee. A trapper usually appears in conjunction with an away block. For example, the blocker on whom the defensive lineman aligns will execute an away block to the left. The defensive lineman closes to his left and throws his eyes through the near hip of the lineman who is blocking away. A defensive lineman must learn to consciously seek some type of action coming back toward him off of an away block. If he learns to expect an opposite-colored jersey coming at him, he can more easily attack the trapper with the proper technique.

What constitutes the proper technique that should be employed for attacking a trapping offensive lineman is a matter of some debate among defensive coaches. Two basic styles of attacking the trapper are used—the spill technique and the squeeze technique. As with most coaching terms, each technique has several aliases. For example, the spill technique is also called the "wrong-shoulder technique," the "cross-arm technique," and the "cross-body technique." The squeeze technique, on the other hand, is commonly referred to as the "right-shoulder technique," the "lead-shoulder technique," and the "outside-leverage technique." The point to keep in mind is that each technique has very specific—and valid—coaching points.

- The defender should turn to face the trapper and attack the trapper with his outside shoulder.
- The defender should drive his outside shoulder to the downfield knee of the trapper. For example, if the trapper is coming from the defensive lineman's left, the defensive lineman should dip his right shoulder to attack the right knee of the blocker in a cross-body type of maneuver.
- The defender's primary goal should be to force a pileup in the running seam.
- The defender should understand that he sacrifices his body and his opportunity to pursue the ballcarrier when he uses the spill technique.
- The linebacker should normally read the pileup and fit next to the pile to make the hit on the ballcarrier.
- The defender should be aware that the individual who "spills" the trap is not responsible for making the tackle on the play; he is only responsible for making a pile, unless he can pry himself through the blocker to the ballcarrier.
- As he masters the techniques involved, the defender should learn to pry through the blocker and get in on the tackle.

Among the coaching points that should be emphasized for the squeeze technique are the following:

- The defender should keep his shoulders parallel to the line of scrimmage (i.e., the defender should never turn to face the trapper).
- The defender should use the edge of his inside shoulder pad to attack the trapper. For example, if the trapper is coming from the defensive lineman's left, the defensive lineman should dip his left shoulder to attack the blocker. This action

allows the defender to keep his shoulders square and his outside arm free.

- The defender's primary goal should be to collapse the running seam by stuffing the trapper back into the hole or stalemating him so that his feet become obstacles for the ballcarrier.
- The defender should stay on his feet, even though he plays near the surface, and should maintain outside leverage to tackle the ballcarrier should he try to bounce out of the seam.
- The linebacker should understand that he is primarily responsible for capping the seam created by the trapper. If the squeeze-technique defender has crushed the trapper, the linebacker should seal the cap and slide outside to fit hip-to-hip with the defensive lineman. If the linebacker sees grass in the seam, it indicates that the squeezing defensive lineman failed to crush the trapper back into the seam. In this situation, the linebacker should continue into the seam to blow up the ballcarrier as he hits the hole behind the trapper. This process is called capping the hole.
- The defender who "squeezes" the trapper should be responsible for making the tackle if the ballcarrier attempts to pop out of the frontside when he sees the linebacker capping the hole.
- The defender who faces a kick-out blocker should move toward the threat and attack the outside knee of the blocker. The defender should never sit and wait for the blocker to come to him. Rather, he should force the blocker to execute his block from a relatively defensive posture, as the defender goes on the attack to the outside knee. Once contact is made with the blocker, the defender should sink his hips and keep his eyes on the ballcarrier. If the ballcarrier is dipping outside, the defender should come off the kick-out block and assist in the tackle. If the ballcarrier rips inside of the kick-out block, two explanations may exist. The defender may have penetrated too deeply into the backfield when he attacked the kick-out blocker, or his interior defensive teammates were soft, thereby allowing massive movement along the offensive scrimmage line and the creation of a great chasm between even the well-played kick-out block and the interior seal of the defensive line. In the second scenario, the defender who is playing the trap has little recourse other than to read the harsh angle of the running back and convert his squeeze technique to a spill technique (knowing that the back is not interested in spilling). This conversion should enable the head-up defensive lineman to rip across the kick-out block, flatten out in his pursuit angle, and possibly stop a big play by the ballcarrier.

The Takeoff

Also referred to as a get-off, the takeoff is closely related to the throwing-the-hands technique. The hands are the initial "rocket launchers" of the defender's body. They provide the impetus to violently thrust the defender's torso and limbs forward. The defender's hips snap forward as his buttocks sink and generate power in his upper body. All of these events occur in a fraction of a second. The takeoff is the catalyst for propelling the defender's body into action—violently and explosively.

On the snap of the ball, the lineman throws the hands, replacing his down-hand with his back foot. This action allows him to take the *big first step*, which is the primary key to an effective takeoff. A big first step may be facilitated by ensuring that every defensive lineman adheres to certain coaching points when the ball moves. Among the personal (coaching-point) factors that a defensive lineman should address during the takeoff are the following:

- The defensive lineman must align on the front tip of the ball (hypothetically, if a credit card can fit between the defender's mask and the ball, he should move closer to the ball).
- He must use a tight, narrow stance.
- He should keep his eyes up.
- He must curl his toes against the grass or turf.
- The defensive lineman should lean into the takeoff.
- He must push and fall out of his stance.
- He should keep his body flexed at 45 degrees.
- The defensive lineman must push down on the front knee with the up-hand.
- He must claw and pull grass with his down-hand.
- He should demonstrate straight-line movement (i.e., no hitches or drawbacks with his hands).

The primary objective of a defensive lineman on his takeoff should be to penetrate and get his head in a crack. The crack-for-the-hat is the gap that corresponds to the defender's leverage arm. In other words, the defensive lineman should take off in a manner that enables him to gain a degree of penetration in the leverage gap. It is not enough for the defender to simply anchor a gap while staying on the line of scrimmage. A defensive lineman must move to get his head in the crack, read the blocking pattern, and react to what is happening by concentrating on the screws on his opponent's helmet. The screws give the defensive lineman the relevant information he needs to continue to respond properly.

4

Defensive Line Play Versus the Pass

Planning for the Pass Rush

The major part of any defensive lineman's job on game day in the National Football League is pass rushing. As a rule, a professional defensive lineman will face pass-protection schemes on more snaps from center than all run-blocking schemes combined. In reality, regardless of the competitive level at which he plays, a defensive lineman should never be surprised by a pass read. He must anticipate that he will have to be a pass rusher on every snap. He should play the pass—and react to the run. To play the pass, a defensive lineman should constantly be aware of the following coaching points for the numerous pass-rush techniques. As a pass rusher, a defensive lineman should:

- Have a plan—An effective pass rusher predetermines his move. Presnap planning of the move increases its quickness factor.
- Maintain a consistent stance—Prior to the snap of the ball, a defensive lineman should crowd the ball and take a good stance, but he shouldn't tip his stance and alert the offensive lineman about where he is going or what move he is going to make.
- Pass rush from a shade alignment—Such an alignment enables a defensive lineman to attack only half the man (his opponent). Forcing an offensive lineman

to commit to one side is often the initial step in making a good move. A shade alignment not only allows the defensive lineman to get his hat in the crack and penetrate, but also forces an offensive lineman to commit to one side.

- Learn to feel the depth of the quarterback's drop—This factor determines the type of pass-rushing technique that is going to be most effective in a particular situation. For example, a short quarterback drop mandates that the defensive lineman execute a quicker pass-rush move (e.g., grab and rip).

- Keep in mind the precept "same hand, same foot"—The primary key to finishing all pass-rushing moves (e.g., slaps, swims, rips) is to have the defensive lineman adhere to the "sand hand, same foot" precept, which states that the defensive lineman should use the same foot as his primary hand to finish a move. For example, when punching his right hand over to perform a swim technique, the defensive lineman should swing his right foot across to gain upfield position on the blocker.

- Use the hands with sharp movements—A pass rusher should visualize his hands as those of a martial arts master. Accordingly, he should use his hands in sharp movements to stun and jerk the offensive lineman. The defender's hands should be wielding a razor, not a sledgehammer.

- Use a counter move when caught (i.e., when the original move did not work)—A defensive lineman should have a counter move to every base pass-rushing move. For example, the counter move for the rip is the rerip or swim.

- Spin or club the blocker when being carried past the quarterback—A pass rusher should never "give up" on his pass rush and allow himself to be carried past the quarterback.

- Keep the weight and momentum going forward toward the quarterback—Above all else, a pass rusher should keep his feet moving and avoid dancing.

- Know the quarterback—The best pass rushers familiarize themselves with a particular quarterback's escape mechanisms. As such, a defensive lineman should use film study (to the extent possible, depending on the specific resources available) to identify the opposing quarterback's escape moves.

- Run through the sack—A pass rusher shouldn't jump or leave his feet to sack the quarterback. He should run through the sack and land on the quarterback, using the quarterback's body to cushion his fall.

The pass-rushing ability of a defensive lineman is enhanced by his practice of the proper get-off technique (refer to Chapter 3). Getting off on the snap with a big step enables a defensive lineman to gain a jump on upfield penetration. All factors considered, dropback pass protection is normally easily recognized by a defender who reads on the run. As the defender replaces his up-hand with his back foot when taking a big step, he reads the screws of the offensive lineman's headgear. If the screws pop up and the offensive lineman shows a "high hat," then the defensive lineman should read dropback pass. An offensive lineman showing a high hat should face a defensive lineman who gets his hat in the crack and attacks the pass-rush lane. Since an attacking read-on-the-run lineman focuses on his get-off and on gaining penetration on every snap, he should never be surprised by a high hat read. He must maintain the mentality of a pass rusher on every down. The defensive coordinator should signal a pass-rushing situation when he is playing a defensive reading scheme with his linemen. This signal allows them to alter their stance, widen a little bit in the gap, and get a better takeoff to rush the passer. If a defensive lineman maintains his balanced, squared-up, basic reading stance, it is very difficult to get a pass rush. A reading lineman must flip his hips and get to an edge when recognizing a high hat, pass-pro set by the offensive lineman.

The Magnificent Seven

As a rule, defensive linemen have seven proven pass-rushing techniques at their disposal. On the other hand, most defensive line coaches feel that their players need to master only a few (i.e., one to three) of these techniques. In reality, a defensive lineman really doesn't need to be accomplished at all seven pass-rushing techniques. In the National Football League, for example, the so-called "sackmasters" usually make their name through the expert use of a single technique.

The Rip Technique

The rip technique is sometimes referred to as speed rush—particularly when it is used by a defensive end. The rip technique involves a defensive lineman dipping the shoulder that is nearest the blocker as he powers past him. The move is initiated by the defender as he uses the hand that is opposite the blocker to pull his near arm forward. The pass rusher should execute such a pull in an explosive, snatching manner. Grabbing and pulling the blocker's near arm enables the rusher to gain an upfield advantage with his outside shoulder. The pass rusher should then rip his leverage arm (i.e., the arm closest to the blocker) upward in the manner of an uppercut to the armpit of the pass blocker, though in reality this uppercut should be directed to a point outside the plane of the blocker's body. Such an uppercut punch is designed to drive the pass blocker's leverage arm upward and force him to turn his shoulders—an action that figuratively opens the gate to the quarterback. (Note: One point that should be strongly emphasized to the pass rusher is that the only time he should raise either hand is when the quarterback has released the ball and the ball is in the defender's path.)

The action of the defender dipping his leverage shoulder also gives the pass protector less blocking surface to contact. The lateral arm (i.e., the arm furthest from the defender's path) really has no available frontal surface to contact. In this instance, the blocker is forced to try to "hip steer" the pass rusher with his lateral arm. The hip-steering technique—a technique that involves the pass protector putting his off-hand on the hip of the speed rusher—is effective on the edge of the line of scrimmage, but not in the interior. The rip technique is suitable for either a defensive tackle or a defensive end and can be made either to the inside or outside of the blocker.

The Swim Technique

The swim technique begins exactly the same way as a rip technique, with a swift slap and grab of the blocker's near shoulder with the defender's offside hand (i.e., the hand opposite the blocker). The offside-hand slap-and-grab aspect of a swim technique is slightly different from the offside-hand slap-and-grab employed in a rip technique. Whereas the rip-technique slap-and-grab is made using a sideways motion (i.e., across the body), in the manner of a roundhouse punch, the offside-hand slap-and-grab of the swim technique is performed with a pulling motion.

When initiating the swim technique, the pass rusher should snap the off-hand downward and grab the blocker on his shoulder—slightly behind the point of the shoulder. Grabbing the blocker's jersey in this manner enables the pass rusher to jerk the near shoulder of the blocker downward. By doing so, the pass rusher gives himself clearance to punch his onside hand (i.e., the hand nearest the blocker) over the depressed (i.e., pulled down) shoulder of the pass protector. A key coaching point regarding this technique is to use the word "punch" to describe the action of the defender's on-hand swinging over the top of the pass protector's depressed shoulder. The word traditionally used to describe this action is "swim" (hence the name given to the technique).

Several knowledgeable defensive coaches have examined the symbolism of using the word "swim" to describe the overhand motion to clear the blocker's shoulder. Because most people visualize a swimmer using a broad, sweeping motion as he reaches to propel himself through the water, many defensive line coaches believe that a more appropriate word to describe the motion of the on-hand in this instance (given its compact, violent nature) is "punch." When learning the swim technique, players should be taught to move their onside hand and onside foot as one body part. Defenders should be encouraged to remember the "same hand, same foot" rule. As the defender's onside hand punches over the depressed shoulder of the pass protector, his onside foot drives to a point near the heel of the blocker's near leg. The defender's objective when driving his foot to the heel of the blocker is to simultaneously get his hip past the blocker's hip. Once the pass rusher's hip has cleared the hip of the blocker, the pass protector cannot recover. The pass rusher can add a final touch to the move by using his on-hand to push off the pass protector's back after he punches his on-hand over and clears the blocker.

The swim move is best used by a taller defensive player on the edge who possesses long limbs and exceptional upper-body strength. It is also an excellent pass-rush move against top-heavy, overly aggressive pass sets.

The Bull Technique

The primary objective of a bull rusher is to elevate the blocker's shoulders and force him back on his heels. Once a defensive lineman reads the high hat and becomes a pass rusher, he should strike the blocker with the heels of his hands. The heels of the rusher's hands should be positioned with the thumbs up, just below the top of the numbers. Using a chuck grasp, the defender should then violently bench press the blocker so that the blocker's shoulders rise, which is a key factor in the success of the bull rush in that it causes the blocker's weight to shift backward. Once such a weight shift is achieved, the defensive lineman has gained a substantial advantage. This type of rush is best when used against a shallow quarterback drop (i.e., a three- or five-step drop). A bull rush is also very effective against a blocker who has set too high, has his weight on his heels, or is floating (i.e., drifting) off of the line of scrimmage.

The Club Technique

As one of the more physical pass-rushing techniques, the club technique is excellent when used by a defensive lineman who possesses both extraordinary upper-body strength and the quick hands of a boxer. When executing a club technique, the pass rusher should sell a vertical push to one side of the blocker. Once the blocker shifts his weight and commits to stopping the rusher's upfield penetration, the pass rusher should then drive his opposite hand into the chest or shoulder of the blocker. The pass rusher's clubbing action is designed to force the blocker toward the direction of his weight shift and to use his own momentum against him. After knocking the blocker off balance with his club hand, the pass rusher should then finish the move by ripping past the blocker with his opposite arm. Like the rip technique, the club technique can be used to beat the blocker either to the inside or to the outside. It is also frequently used by defensive linemen to set up counter moves. As such, the club technique is one of the most effective rushes in the National Football League—one that is widely employed by both defensive ends and defensive tackles.

The Spin Technique

An effective technique for defensive linemen at any level, the spin technique offers several advantages, including—depending on the circumstances—providing an opportunity for a quicker, less-physical pass rusher to dominate a bigger, stronger offensive lineman. More than any other technique, however, the spin technique enables a defensive lineman to use his shoulder. To execute a spin move, the pass rusher drives upfield to a point immediately outside the near shoulder of the blocker. The offensive lineman will usually respond by leaning into the pass rusher to maximize his weight advantage. At the point where the pass rusher feels the pass protector shifting his weight into the block, the pass rusher should plant his foot nearest the blocker.

As he plants his near foot, the pass rusher should take advantage of the momentum of his onside shoulder by using his onside hand and arm to shove the blocker in the direction of the pass rusher's momentum. While shoving the blocker with his onside arm, the pass rusher should sharply swing his offside elbow rearward. Swinging the elbow opens the pass rusher's shoulders and hips so that he can drop step around to hook the back of the blocker's leg. The pass rusher has thus pinned the pass protector. The pass rusher should then complete his spin and work to regain an appropriate degree of leverage on track to the quarterback's passing arm and shoulder. The spin technique is a very effective pass-rushing technique for the defensive end, and can be used by the tackle against an offensive guard who employs a wide set.

The Shake-and-Bake Technique

The shake-and-back technique is a great pass-rushing method for a defensive lineman who enjoys a significant advantage in quickness and speed over his opponent. The shake-and-bake technique essentially involves a situation in which a defender "pretends" to be a running back or wide receiver. The pass rusher simply uses his best move(s) to fake-out the pass protector and pressure the quarterback. As such, the shake-and-bake technique is best used from the edge, where the pass rusher has a lot of room in which to operate. In recent years, this technique has been widely used by blitzing linebackers, safeties, and cornerbacks. The shake-and-back move is an excellent change-up technique for a quick defensive end to use on an obvious passing down. It must be executed as close to the blocker as possible.

The Push-Pull Technique

A complementary technique to the bull technique, the push-pull technique is a fundamentally simple move that can be most effectively used by a pass rusher who is able to maintain a relatively low center of gravity. An effective bull technique is designed to enable a pass rusher to stun and lift the pass protector. After stunning the blocker, the pass rusher finishes his bull technique with an explosively strong bench press. Using his chuck grasp to grab the blocker just below the top of the numbers, the pass rusher quickly jerks the off-balance pass protector toward him, releases him, and clears the blocker.

The push-pull technique is a very effective complement to the bull technique that can be utilized in the interior line. It is an especially appropriate technique for use at the lower levels of competition, where young offensive linemen frequently tip their weight forward when pass blocking. The push-pull technique uses the pass blocker's tendency to overextend against him.

Sacking the Quarterback

Ideally, the defensive lineman should always use a draping technique when sacking the quarterback. In other words, whenever possible, the pass rusher should bring both of his arms down on the shoulders of the quarterback as he makes contact. A pass rusher should use his outside arm to hook the elbow of the quarterback's passing arm as the quarterback cocks his arm in the throwing movement. By draping his arms downward on the passer, the defender is able to prevent the last-second release of the ball by the quarterback. The draping sack technique also helps a pass rusher finish sacking an agile quarterback who is attempting to duck under him. By being under control and by draping the quarterback, the defender is able to smother an up-and-under "duck" move by the quarterback. The draping technique prevents the defender's forward momentum from carrying him past the quarterback when he steps up to duck under the pass rusher.

The pass rusher should always rush toward the passer's back shoulder with the intention of sacking him from the outside-in. If possible, the defender should chop downward with his outside arm on the quarterback's passing arm, trying to create the fumble and, hopefully, a great turnover.

Pass Rushing From the Defensive End Position

The degree to which a defensive end should be responsible for containment in passing situations is a matter that is often a debate among coaches. The question arises because, depending upon the defensive coaching philosophies, a defensive end is often asked to do two separate tasks—contain the quarterback and provide a pass rush. The debated issue usually involves establishing the relative priority of containment versus pressure. Many coaches feel that the defensive end should not be asked to contain if he is to pressure the quarterback. In the professional ranks, most coaches place the primary emphasis on the pass-rush responsibility of the defensive end.

All factors considered, the minimum number of defensive linemen that can consistently pressure the quarterback is four. Since a four-man line is the most common defensive alignment employed in the National Football League, the professional defensive end is expected to pressure the quarterback first—and contain second. Even when teaching in a system that utilizes five defensive linemen, the defensive coach who preaches containment instead of pressure will typically get a tentative pass rush from the edge. Certainly, an argument can be advanced that, if only four pass rushers are available, the philosophy of containment on the edge is a luxury that most coaches cannot afford.

The best pass-rushing strategy for a defensive end is often the most basic—the jet technique. The jet alignment is simply a wide alignment that facilitates a wide speed rush. Gap protection schemes that shut down the inside stunts and pass-rushing lanes should not be able to hold up against a defensive end that utilizes a jet technique. In fact, the success of an inside stunting game, for example, is dependent upon the threat of the outside rush.

A jet technique is the basic speed-rush technique on which the entire premise of pressuring the quarterback is based. In the jet technique, a speed-rushing defensive end sprints approximately three yards deep into the backfield, at the point at which he recognizes dropback pass protection. It is important to emphasize that the defensive end should keep his initial path vertical and should not close in distance to the pass protector. Rushing to an outside point (some three yards deep) is designed to force a pass protector to bucket step with his outside foot and open his hips. In these situations, the pass protector must compensate with this move if he did not kick off the line of scrimmage in anticipation of a speed rush. When the pass protector bucket steps, he puts his inside foot in a position that is a wide straddle distance from his outside foot. As such, he loses power base and, thus, loses his ability to react quickly.

If an offensive tackle is beaten by an initial speed-rush charge, the defensive end will gain an uphill advantage on the blocker. Beating an offensive tackle to the three-yard point is called gaining the high ground. Once the high ground is obtained, the defensive end should angle inward toward the back shoulder of the quarterback. While going for the back shoulder makes the defensive end vulnerable to the duck-and-under move by the quarterback, this point is the appropriate landmark for the defensive end's dual responsibility of pressure and containment. Furthermore, if the defensive end misses the sack, the quarterback will normally step up and under into the defensive tackle's pass-rush lane. The point that should be emphasized is that the defensive end should never be in a situation where he misses the sack and has the quarterback spin out to the outside of the defensive rush.

A defensive end should tackle the quarterback high, using a draping type of tackle. The draping technique, however, is not as exaggerated at the defensive end position as it is for defensive tackles. If rushing from the defensive right, the defensive end should attempt to gain the high ground and aim for the back shoulder of the quarterback—the right shoulder of a right-handed quarterback. As the defensive end makes contact on the sack, for example, his right arm should chop down on the throwing arm of the quarterback. If the quarterback is attempting to throw, the right defensive end's right arm should hook the elbow of his throwing arm. The defensive end should the slash his arm down the quarterback's throwing arm to knock the ball loose. The chop should always be delivered to the elbow of the quarterback's throwing arm, not to his hand. If the defensive end chops down at the ball and misses, he will typically contact nothing but the air behind the quarterback. On the other hand, if the defender's chop hooks the quarterback's arm above his elbow, the ball is often stripped from the quarterback's grasp.

If the quarterback catches sight of a defensive end, he will usually bring the ball down to his side in a loose tuck or in an extension away from his body. By chopping the quarterback's throwing arm, the defensive end can hook the extended arm of the quarterback. Once the chopping hand of the defensive end grasps the quarterback's throwing arm in such a scenario, the defensive end should jerk the quarterback's elbow toward his body. This action will normally force the quarterback's arm backward. As a result, the ball—exposed and unprotected—will cock outward from the quarterback's body.

The offside hand of a defensive end should be swung toward the quarterback—somewhat in the manner of a roundhouse punch. Such a punch is designed to corral the quarterback as he attempts to step up. The pass rusher's offside arm should be swung at chest level at the quarterback. If the quarterback attempts to duck, the defender's offside arm should be used to grasp the ducking quarterback in an attempt to keep him from escaping. A coaching point that should be emphasized is to make sure that the defensive end keeps his offside hand open. If he grasps the helmet of a ducking quarterback, he may come in contact with the quarterback's facemask and be penalized.

Pass Rushing From the Defensive Tackle Position

The critical factor in a defensive tackle's effectiveness as a pass rusher is penetration. Regardless of whether he is running a stunt or just making a one-on-one move, a defensive tackle must get his hat in the crack. The relative success of any inside stunts performed by a defensive tackle depends on his ability to get off on the snap and penetrate. By pushing a point through the offensive line, the defensive tackle can either force a double-team or cause the blocker to turn his shoulders and open the gate to the quarterback. In fact, the primary objective of the nose guard in some defensive alignments is to force a double-team between the center and the near guard.

The best defensive tackle move is the slap and rip. When this move is employed, the defensive tackle uses his leverage hand to slap the triceps of the blocker's near arm and knock the arm sideways or downward. A defensive tackle should remember to use a "razor" and not a "sledgehammer" to quickly snap a blocker's shoulder down and inward. The pass rusher should immediately use an uppercut punching motion to rip the opposite arm across the blocker's face, while gaining the upfield advantage by swinging the foot corresponding to the ripping arm across the blocker's body (i.e., the "same hand, same foot" rule).

Other commonly used moves that have also been effective for the defensive tackle in many situations are the rip-rerip counter move and the push-pull move. In both situations, it is important to emphasize that a defensive tackle should get his hands on the blocker. Although offensive guards are usually extremely physical, they tend to get more forward lean in their technique. This lean occurs because the blockers face an ongoing effort to penetrate their ranks by the opposing defensive tackles. By using his hands to punch and control the offensive guard, a defensive tackle can use the guard's mission as a stop-gap blocker against him. If the guard begins to get top heavy after a few downs of pass protection, the defensive tackle can blow by him with the push-pull move. But without using a good technique with his hands on every down, the defensive lineman would never know that the prime time for the push-pull move has arrived. This match would continue essentially as a head-butting slugfest in the middle. If a defensive tackle can't get his head in the crack or use his hands properly, he will not be able to apply much pressure up the middle.

Similar to the situation with the defensive ends, individual tackle pass-rush techniques are best employed from a jet-technique alignment. It is the responsibility of defensive coaches to make sure that they provide opportunities for their defensive tackles to set up in a jet alignment, not only on the passing downs, but also on running downs. While a shadow alignment is also a good alignment from which to jet, a jet alignment for a defensive tackle is designed to give the tackle slightly more leverage than a shadow alignment. The jetting 3-technique defensive tackle, for example, can widen to a point where his anchor foot is toe-to-toe with the blocker's *outside* foot. A jetting 1-technique defender, on the other hand, can widen to a point where his anchor foot is toe-to-toe with the blocker's *inside* foot.

Technique Play Against Common Blocking Schemes

The 1-2-3 technique-numbering system for specifying where a defensive lineman should be positioned prior to the snap of the ball relative to an offensive lineman is discussed in detail in Chapter 2. In this system, the defensive lineman may align in one of three basic alignments over an offensive lineman.

1 Technique

This technique is an inside alignment on an offensive lineman, including the tight end and slotback. The 1-technique defender's anchor foot is his outside foot. His responsible gap is the nearest inside gap. The three possible 1-technique positioning variations are the shade, crotch, and shadow alignments. The shade 1 technique puts the defender's outside foot on the outside plane of the offensive lineman's stance, while the crotch 1 technique places his outside foot on the midline plane of the offensive lineman's stance. In the shadow 1 technique, the defender's outside foot is positioned on the inside plane of the offensive lineman's stance. Diagrams 5-1 through 5-3 illustrate examples of the shade, crotch, and shadow 1-technique alignments, respectively, against an offensive guard.

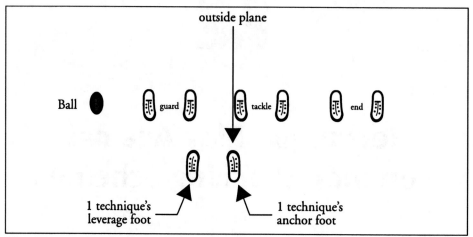

Diagram 5-1. The shade 1-technique alignment on the offensive guard

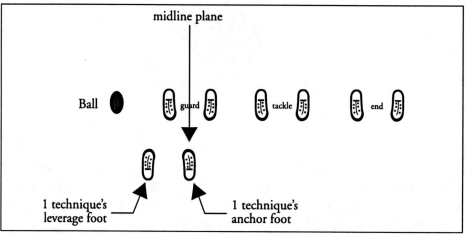

Diagram 5-2. The crotch 1-technique alignment on the offensive guard

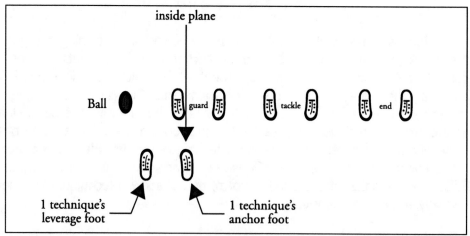

Diagram 5-3. The shadow 1-technique alignment on the offensive guard

2 Technique

This technique is a head-up alignment on an offensive lineman, including the tight end and slotback. If the 2 technique is a one-gap player, his anchor foot is the outside foot. The one-gap 2 technique places his anchor foot directly in front of the outside foot of the blocker. The one-gap 2 technique's responsible gap is the nearest inside gap. In this situation, he should consciously work to keep his inside arm free in his responsible gap. If the 2 technique is a two-gap player, he will attack the blocker and bench press away from his body as he fights the pressure and pursues the ballcarrier. Since the 2 technique is in a head-up (i.e., toe-to-toe) alignment, no shade, crotch, or shadow alignment variations exist. Diagram 5-4 illustrates an example of a one-gap 2-technique defender aligned on an offensive tackle.

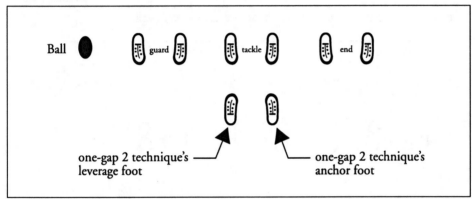

Diagram 5-4. The one-gap 2 technique alignment on the offensive tackle

3 Technique

This technique is an inside alignment on an offensive lineman, including the tight end and slotback. The 3-technique defender's anchor foot is his inside foot. His responsible gap is the nearest outside gap. Like the 1 technique, the three possible 3-technique positioning variations are the shade, crotch, and shadow alignments. In the shade 3 technique, the defender puts his inside foot on the inside plane of the offensive lineman's stance. In the crotch 3 technique, he places his inside foot on the midline plane of the offensive lineman's stance. In the shadow 3 technique, the defender puts his inside foot on the outside plane of the offensive lineman's stance. Diagrams 5-5 through 5-7 show a shade, crotch, and shadow 3-technique alignment, respectively, against a tight end.

Regardless of the technique alignment in which he is positioned, a defender must be able to react properly to whatever blocking pattern he is facing and discharge his basic responsibilities on a given play. The primary focus of this chapter is to present an overview discussion of how 1, 2, and 3 techniques should react to each type of block.

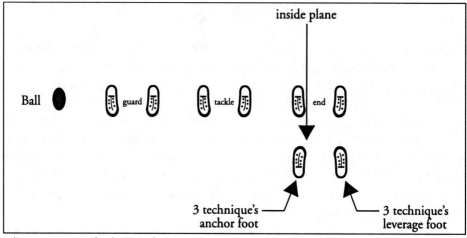

Diagram 5-5. A shade 3 technique alignment on the tight end

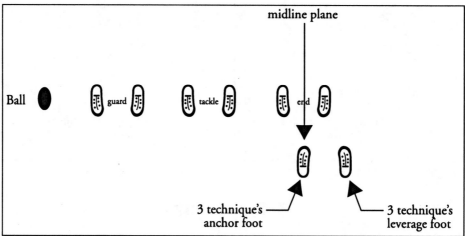

Diagram 5-6. A crotch 3 technique alignment on the tight end

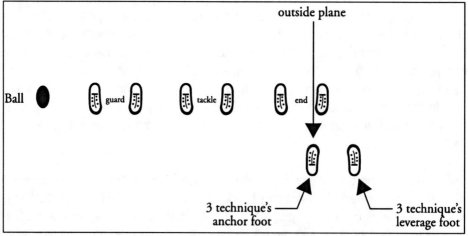

Diagram 5-7. A shadow 3 technique alignment on the tight end

It should be noted that since the one-gap technique is a head-up technique—but still an inside technique alignment—the 2 technique faces basically the same blocking patterns as the 1 technique. Because the standard alignment of each technique is the crotch alignment, all of the defensive reactions that are discussed and diagrammed in this chapter refer to the crotch alignment unless otherwise specified.

Defeating a Drive Block

To defeat a drive block, a defensive lineman should take off on movement and explode upfield with a big first step. He should get his hat in the crack and maintain leverage in the inside gap. Regardless of his alignment technique, the defensive lineman should be taught to create a wreck in the gap versus a drive block.

Whenever a defensive lineman is aligned in either a 1 or 2 technique, he should use the shoulder-blow delivery method of attacking the blocker. Once the defender stuns the blocker with his outside shoulder, he should bench press the blocker and control him. If the ball is hitting up the gut, both the 1 and 2 technique should attempt to create a bubble in the offensive line and force the ballcarrier to search for a seam in the defense. If the ball is going wide, the defensive lineman who is aligned in either a 1 or 2 technique should use his outside arm to pull the blocker to the inside as he rips his inside arm in a tight uppercut motion across the offensive lineman's body. This push-rip combination allows the defender to cross the face of the blocker and pursue the football. Diagrams 5-8 and 5-9 illustrate how a defensive tackle who is aligned in a 1 or 2 technique, respectively, should react to a drive block.

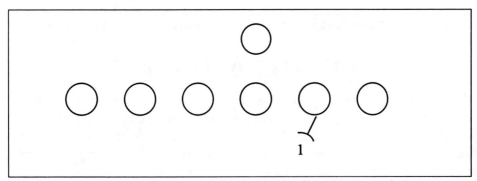

Diagram 5-8. A drive block versus a defensive tackle aligned in a 1 technique

On the other hand, if a defensive lineman is aligned in a 3 technique, he should attack the blocker by bench pressing him and pushing him into the inside gap. The 3-technique defender should keep his shoulders square as he stuffs the blocker into the hole. If the ball is hitting in the A gap, the 3-technique defensive guard, for example, should buckle the offensive guard's knees and drive him down inside so that a bubble is created in the offensive line. Similar to the actions of the 1 technique and the 2

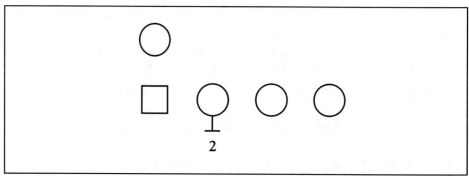

Diagram 5-9. A drive block versus a defensive guard aligned in a 2 technique

technique, this scenario is designed to force the ballcarrier to search for a seam in the defense. If the ball is going wide, the defensive lineman in a 3 technique should use his inside arm to push off the blocker and pursue flat down to the line. Diagram 5-10 illustrates a drive block against a defensive guard aligned in a 3 technique.

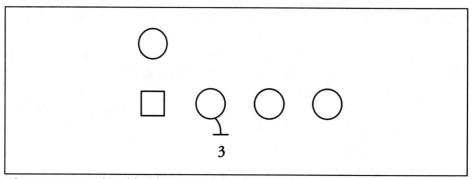

Diagram 5-10. A drive block versus a defensive guard aligned in a 3 technique

Defeating a Turnout Block

Given the fact that both the 1 technique and 2 technique involve an inside alignment, a defensive lineman positioned in either alignment should never be turned out. To defeat the turnout block, a defender in either a 1 or 2 technique should explode upfield with a big first step and get his hat in the crack of the inside gap. Whenever a defensive lineman is aligned in either a 1 or 2 technique, he should use the shoulder-blow delivery method of attacking the blocker. Once he stuns the blocker with his outside shoulder, the defensive lineman should bench press the blocker and control him. The defender should then flatten the turnout block and make the tackle on the ballcarrier. Diagrams 5-11 and 5-12 illustrate a turnout block versus a defender aligned in a 1 technique and a 2 technique, respectively.

Against a turnout block, the 3 technique should explode off the ball and attack the outside "V" landmark on the blocker. The primary responsibility of the 3 technique

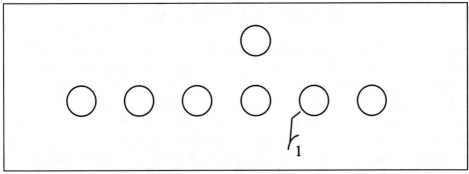

Diagram 5-11. A turnout block versus a defensive guard aligned in a 1 technique

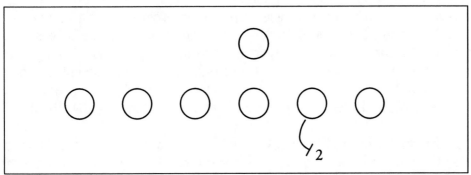

Diagram 5-12. A turnout block versus a defensive tackle aligned in a 2 technique

against a turnout block is to squeeze the inside gap and maintain leverage until he is sure the ball is hitting to his inside. Once the 3 technique determines with 100 percent certainty that the ball is hitting to his inside, he should use his arm to pull himself across the blocker's face. The 3 technique should never turn his shoulders when he feels a turnout block. He should remain in a snug fit to the blocker's headgear until he determines that he should rip across the blocker's face. Diagram 5-13 illustrates a turnout block against a defensive end aligned in a 3 technique.

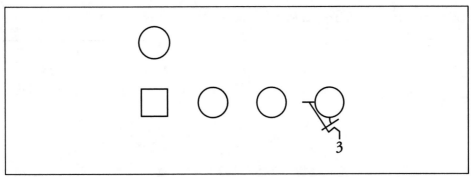

Diagram 5-13. A turnout block versus a defensive end aligned in a 3 technique

Defeating a Hook Block

Against a hook block, a defensive lineman utilizing either a 1 technique or a 2 technique is essentially beaten by alignment. Despite being outflanked, such a defender can accomplish several objectives against a hook block, particularly with regard to the defensive end–tight end match-up. Against a hook block, a defender aligned in either a 1 or 2 technique should take off on the snap and get his head in the crack of the inside gap. He should also use the shoulder-blow delivery method of attacking the blocker. Once he stuns the blocker with his outside shoulder, he should bench press the blocker and control him. The defender should then push through the blocker's inside shoulder and run through the gap. Once through the gap, the defensive player must flatten his line of pursuit to avoid running a fishhook in the backfield. Diagrams 5-14 and 5-15 illustrate a hook block against a defensive tackle aligned in a 1 technique and a 2 technique, respectively. If penetration through the gap is not possible, the defender should stalemate the blocker and attempt to stretch his block outward three to five yards. It is important for the defender to realize that he should never allow himself to be pushed off the line of scrimmage by a hook block.

On the other hand, against a hook block, a 3-technique defender must never allow himself to be hooked. If a 3-technique defender is consistently hooked, the integrity of the defensive scheme will eventually collapse. The key to a 3 technique defeating a

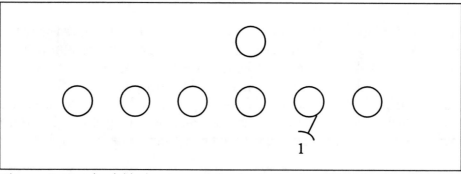

Diagram 5-14. A hook block versus a defensive tackle aligned in a 1 technique

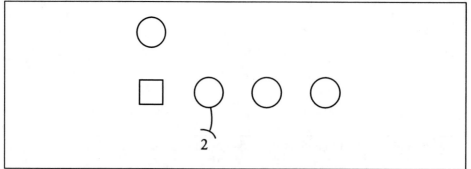

Diagram 5-15. A hook block versus a defensive guard aligned in a 2 technique

hook block is a big first step. If he takes off on the snap and gets his hat in the crack, the 3 technique will beat a hook block. While an offensive lineman has to make an over-and-up move to strike his hook-block landmark, a defensive lineman only has to explode upfield on the snap. All factors considered, the 3 technique enjoys a natural advantage over the hook-blocking lineman due to his outside alignment. Accordingly, defensive linemen should be made to understand how to effectively use this advantage. As such, the importance of a 3 technique taking a big first step against the hook block must be emphasized. How a defender responds after dealing with a hook block is relatively dependent on the defensive position he plays. For example, a defensive end releases off the tight end and attempts to execute a hook block with more of an upfield pursuit angle than either a defensive tackle or a guard would employ against a blocker. Furthermore, the tighter the 3 technique aligns to the ball, the flatter his outside pursuit angle should be, once he uses his inside hand to push off the blocker. Diagram 5-16 illustrates a hook block against a 3-technique defender.

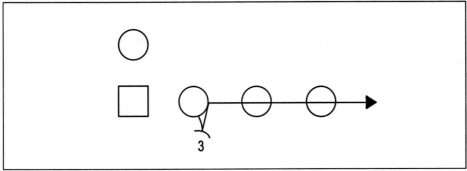

Diagram 5-16. A hook block versus a defensive guard aligned in a 3 technique

Defeating an Outside-Cylinder Hook Block

An outside-cylinder hook block is a hook block in which the blocker takes a wide-position step in an attempt to seal the defensive lineman inside. This type of block is sometimes used after the offensive lineman has unsuccessfully attempted to hook block. When not used as a compensatory technique, the outside-cylinder hook block is used as a means of blocking the plays that involve the ballcarrier attempting to quickly get around the edge. To counter the outside-cylinder hook block, a defensive lineman must drive through the blocker's inside shoulder and penetrate the gap. This action is accomplished by the defensive lineman getting off on the snap with a big first step and getting his hat in the crack of the inside gap. Once the defensive lineman gains the upfield leverage on the outside-cylinder hook blocker, he should flatten out his line of pursuit to get to the ballcarrier.

As a general rule, a defender aligned in either a 1 or 2 technique must lose some ground to wheel backdoor after he gains the upfield advantage. Defeating the outside-cylinder hook block requires that a defensive 1 technique or 2 technique execute the finish of a swim move as he penetrates the gap. Accordingly, a defensive lineman aligned in either a 1 or 2 technique must get his outside foot to a position near the heel of the blocker's inside foot. Getting the outside foot to this position guarantees that the defender will achieve clearance of the opponent's blocking surface. Diagrams 5-17 and 5-18 illustrate an outside-cylinder hook block against a 1 technique and a 2 technique defensive guard, respectively.

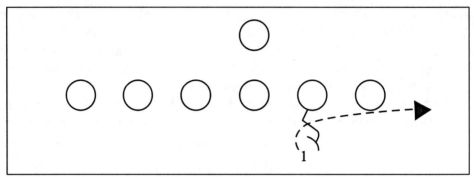

Diagram 5-17. An outside-cylinder hook block versus a defensive guard aligned in a 1 technique

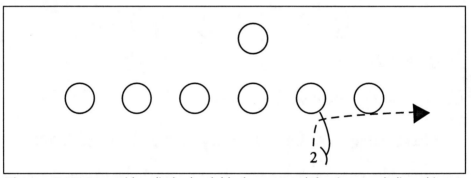

Diagram 5-18. An outside-cylinder hook block versus a defensive guard aligned in a 2 technique

The reactions of a 3-technique defender against an outside-cylinder block are somewhat different than those required for either a 1 technique or a 2 technique. The 3 technique should fight to maintain outside leverage. If the blocker manages to gain the advantage of outside leverage on him, the 3-technique defender should ride the blocker outward to flatten his path. In the case of the blocker initially gaining an advantage, the defender should attempt to turn the blocker's shoulders and fight outside. In flattening the blocker, the 3 technique should look to locate the ballcarrier and take an appropriate pursuit angle. If necessary, the leveraged 3 technique should break behind the buttocks of the outside-cylinder blocker to regain proper position on the ballcarrier. Pursuing behind a flattened outside-cylinder block is an effective technique.

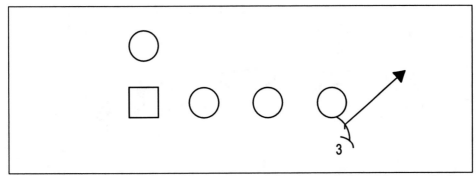

Diagram 5-19. An outside hook block versus a defensive end aligned in a 3 technique

Defeating an Easy Block

Also called an arc release block, an easy block can be employed by an offensive team as a form of bait for a trap play. As a rule, however, an easy block is typically executed by the tight end.

A defender (e.g., the defensive end) aligned with a 1 technique should get off on the snap and find the screws. In this situation, the defensive end should initially play an easy block as he would play a hook block. He should step to push through the inside shoulder of the blocker. Once he feels the blocker arc release, the defensive end should push off the blocker and close down to the inside.

An important coaching point states that the defensive end's inside recovery step to close must be a flat step. If the defender steps upfield with his inside foot as he closes, he will open a crease between himself and the interior. All factors considered, this block is easily played if the defensive end learns to throw his eyes to the inside anytime he recognizes the initial move of either the hook block or easy block. The defensive end doesn't need to look at a hook-blocking tight end to defeat him.

Once the defensive end (aligned in a 1, 2, or 3 technique) recognizes the blocker's intention, he should get his eyes inside to find the ballcarrier as he defeats the blocker. Against an easy block, the defensive end should hurry to close off the C gap. If he recognizes that a pulling lineman is on a trap angle toward him, he should attack the inside knee of the trapper using the wrong-shoulder technique (refer to Chapter 3). Whenever the defensive end reads trap, his objective should be to spill the play. Diagrams 5-20 and 5-21 illustrate an easy block against a 1-technique and a 2-technique defensive end, respectively.

An easy block is frequently issued again the 3-technique defensive end. Similar to a defender aligned in either a 1 or 2 technique, the 3-technique defensive end should get off on the snap and find the screws. Furthermore, the 3-technique defensive end

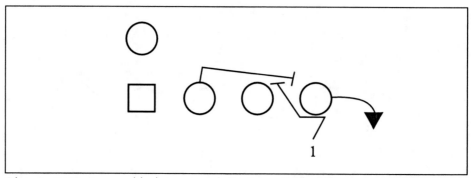

Diagram 5-20. An easy block versus a defensive end aligned in a 1 technique

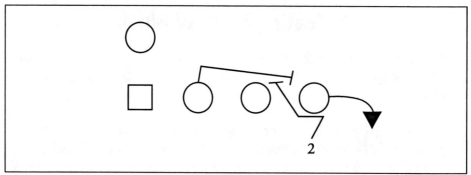

Diagram 5-21. An easy block versus a defensive end aligned in a 2 technique

should initially play the easy block as he would play a hook block. As he reads the tight end attempting to slip across his face, the 3-technique defensive end feels the arc release.

One way for the defensive end to recognize the difference between an easy block and a cylinder hook block is to notice the eyes and shoulders of the tight end. If a tight end is arc releasing, his eyes will be looking upfield to the next level of defenders, and his shoulders will turn to the sideline. A hook-blocking tight end will keep his eyes on the defensive end, and his shoulders will be facing more toward the line of scrimmage. Once the 3-technique defensive end feels an arc release, he should use his outside arm to push off the blocker and close down to the inside.

Again, an important coaching point that should be emphasized is that the 3-technique defensive end's inside recovery step to close must be a flat step. If the defender steps upfield with his inside foot as he closes, he will open a crease between himself and the interior. All factors considered, an arc release is easily played if the defensive end learns to throw his eyes to the inside anytime he recognizes the upfield focus of the tight end who has tilted his shoulders. As such, the defensive end doesn't need to look at a hook-blocking tight end to defeat him. Diagram 5-22 illustrates an easy block against a 3-technique defensive end.

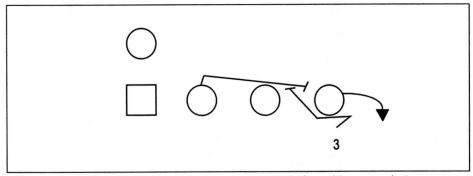

Diagram 5-22. An easy block versus a defensive end aligned in a 3 technique

Technique Play Against an Inside Release

Down Block

For a defender aligned in either a 1 technique or 2 technique, a down block looks exactly like a drive block. To react properly to a down block, the defender should get off on the snap with the big step and find the screws. The technique used to play the down block from either a 1 technique or 2 technique alignment is the same as the technique used to play a drive block. The defender should use the shoulder-blow delivery method of attacking the down blocker. Once the defender buckles the knees of the blocker with his outside shoulder, he should bench press the blocker, control him, and fight pressure with pressure. Against a down block by an interior lineman, the defensive tackle aligned in a 1 technique or 2 technique should prevent the down blocker from getting inside. He should also close to either make the hit on the ballcarrier or defeat the trapping guard. As a rule, a down block by either an offensive guard or tackle is associated with some type of trap. The defensive tackle should use the wrong-shoulder technique to attack the pulling guard and spill the trap.

Against a down block by the tight end, a defensive end aligned in a 1, 2, or 3 technique should find the ball and, if appropriate, squeeze to make the tackle. A down block by the tight end against a defensive end is usually associated with the counter trey play (i.e., counter O-Y play). In this situation, the defender should force the counter trey ballcarrier to run the bubble around the penetration of the defensive end. If the lead blocker on the counter trey play attempts to kick-out the defensive end aligned in a 1 or 2 technique, the defender should use his outside shoulder to attack the inside knee of the trap blocker and spill the play.

A 3-technique defender should react to a down block in a maneuver similar to both a 1-technique and 2-technique defensive lineman. Diagrams 5-23 through 5-25 illustrate a down block against a defender aligned in a 1 technique, a 2 technique, and a 3 technique, respectively.

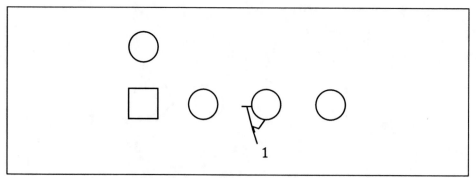

Diagram 5-23. A down block versus a defensive tackle aligned in a 1 technique

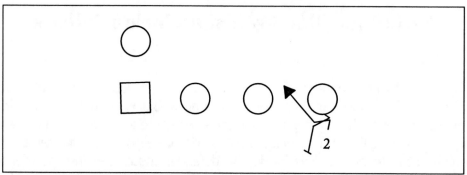

Diagram 5-24. A down block versus a defensive end aligned in a 2 technique

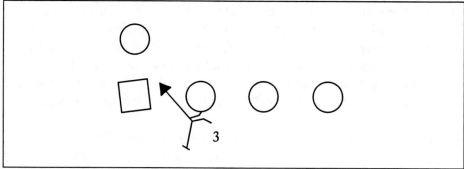

Diagram 5-25. A down block versus a defensive guard aligned in a 3 technique

Technique Play Against the Offside Pull

"Y" Pull

The "Y" pull (i.e., a tight-end pull) is used with the counter "O-Y" play, which is a counter trey play that involves the backside tight end pulling instead of the backside tackle. A "pull" generally dictates a "collision." In other words, if an offensive player pulls away from a defender, the defender should attempt to make contact with him, or at least get in his hip pocket and slash down the line of scrimmage to make the tackle.

The maneuver in which a 1-technique, 2-technique, and 3-technique defender should react to a "Y" pull is basically the same. Against a tight-end pull, the defensive end

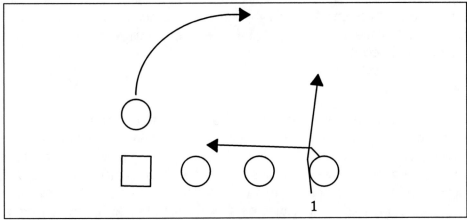

Diagram 5-26. A "Y" pull versus a defensive end aligned in a 1 technique

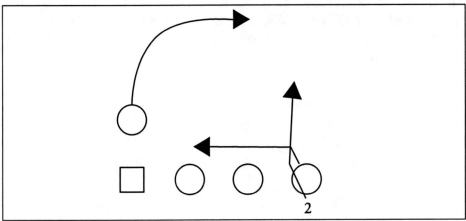

Diagram 5-27. A "Y" pull versus a defensive end aligned in a 2 technique

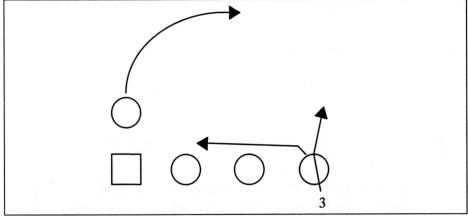

Diagram 5-28. A "Y" pull versus a defensive end aligned in a 3 technique

should immediately gain ground upfield and contain. A defensive end should never be surprised by a play-action pass or bootleg. Whenever the tight end pulls to the opposite side, the defensive end should shoot his eyes inside to the quarterback and play on the arc from his back shoulder. A tight-end pull is a bootleg read. Diagrams 5-26 through 5-28 illustrate a "Y" pull against a defensive end aligned in a 1 technique, 2 technique, and 3 technique, respectively.

"T" Pull

The "T" pull (i.e., the offensive tackle pull) is used with a counter trey play. Whenever an interior defender (1, 2, or 3 technique) who is aligned on the offensive tackle reads an offside pull, he should get in the hip pocket of the pulling tackle and run a flat path down the line of scrimmage. Regardless of whether he is positioned in a 1, 2, or 3 technique, an interior defender aligned on an offensive tackle shouldn't play bootleg when he reads an offside pull. Rather, he should attempt to disrupt the timing of the play by making contact with the pulling tackle (i.e., "collisioning" him). The defender aligned on an offensive tackle should attempt to get his hands on the tackle to physically impede the offensive player's efforts to pull to the opposite side. Diagrams 5-29 and 5-30 illustrate a defensive tackle aligned against a 1 technique and a 2 technique, respectively.

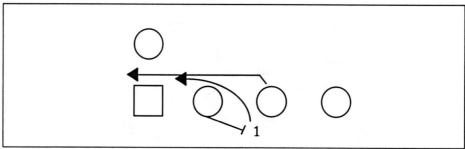

Diagram 5-29. A "T" pull versus a defensive tackle aligned in a 1 technique

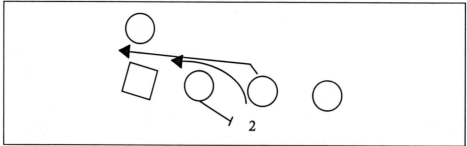

Diagram 5-30. A "T" pull versus a defensive tackle aligned in a 2 technique

The reaction requirements for a 3-technique defender against a "T" pull, while somewhat similar to those for both a 1-technique and a 2-technique defender, involve at least one significant difference. When a 3-technique tackle reads the "T" pull, he will usually get a running back coming at him from an inside-out angle. If the running back is coming low, as on a Bill-O block, the 3-technique defender should get his outside pad and his hands down to protect himself. If the running back is coming high, the running back is probably attempting to slip out into the flat of a bootleg fake. In that situation, the defender should attack the running back and knock him to the ground so that he can't get out into the pass pattern. Diagram 5-31 illustrates a "T" pull against a 3-technique defensive tackle.

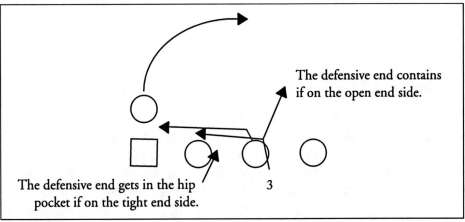

The defensive end contains if on the open end side.

The defensive end gets in the hip pocket if on the tight end side.

3

Diagram 5-31. A "T" pull versus a defensive tackle aligned in a 3 technique

"G" Pull

The "G" pull (i.e., the offensive guard pull) is used with the counter trey play, as well as other types of trap plays (e.g., quick trap, long trap, bootleg). A 1-technique and 2-technique defensive guard aligned on the offensive guard play the "G" pull in exactly the same manner as a 3 technique plays a fold block. A "G" pull block is played exactly like a fold block because a "G" block read will always be accompanied by a fold block from the center. When reacting to a "G" pull, the defensive guard aligned in either a 1 technique or a 2 technique gets off on the ball and explodes upfield with his big first step. He gets his head in the A-gap crack and finds the screws of the center's headgear. The defender should drop his inside shoulder and wheel backdoor to make the play. To do so, the defender must flatten his path down the line of scrimmage. The coaching

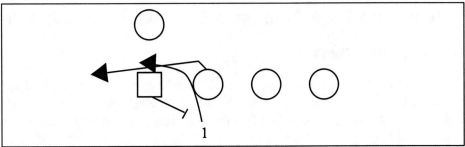

1

Diagram 5-32. A "G" pull versus a defensive guard aligned in a 1 technique points of playing the "G" pull and the "T" pull are essentially identical. Diagrams 5-32 and 5-33 illustrate a "G" pull against a defensive guard aligned in a 1 technique and a 2 technique, respectively.

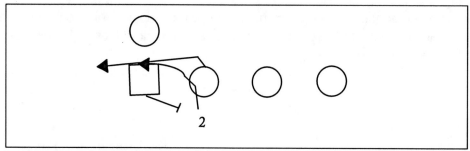

Diagram 5-33. A "G" pull versus a defensive guard aligned in a 2 technique

The reactions required of a 3-technique defensive guard against a "G" pull are slightly different than those involved for either a 1-technique or 2-technique defender. Most of the differences emanate from the fact that a reach block from the offensive tackle is much more common than a fold-block combination against a 3-technique defensive guard. Accordingly, when the 3-technique defensive guard reads a "G" pull, he should lower his outside pad to protect himself against the cutting technique of the offensive tackle's reach block. The defender should use his outside pad to ricochet off the offensive tackle's reach block and then continue inside on a relatively flat path down the line of scrimmage. Diagram 5-34 illustrates a "G" pull against a defensive guard aligned in a 3 technique.

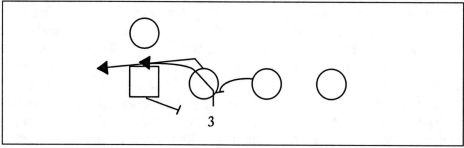

Diagram 5-34. A "G" pull versus a defensive guard aligned in a 3 technique

Technique Play Against a Dropback Pass Block

Tight End Dropback Pass Block

The reactions by a 1-, 2-, or 3-technique defensive end against a tight end's dropback pass block are essentially the same. The 1-technique defensive end should explode upfield with a big initial step after reading the high hat. The defensive end's primary objective should be to close the distance between himself and the tight end. Ideally, a defensive end wants to set up an outside move and turn the edge on the tight end.

Since a 1-technique defensive end operates from an inside presnap alignment, while a 2 technique is positioned in a head-up alignment, both defenders must work hard to gain outside leverage on a pass-blocking tight end. On the other hand, because a 3-technique defensive end operates from an outside presnap alignment, he has a presnap advantage in gaining the outside leverage on a pass-blocking tight end. Diagrams 5-35 through 5-37 illustrate a tight end's dropback pass block against a defensive end aligned in a 1 technique, 2 technique, and 3 technique, respectively.

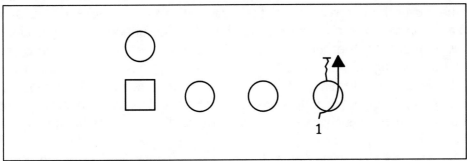

Diagram 5-35. A tight end's dropback pass block versus a defensive end aligned in a 1 technique

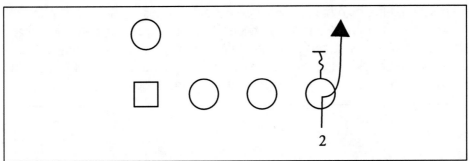

Diagram 5-36. A tight end's dropback pass block versus a defensive end aligned in a 2 technique

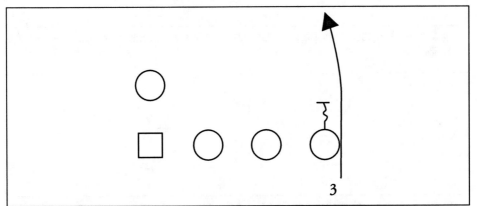

Diagram 5-37. A tight end's dropback pass block versus a defensive end aligned in a 3 technique

Tackle Dropback Pass Block

Versus a tackle's dropback pass block, the reaction responsibilities of a 1-technique and 2-technique defensive tackle are essentially the same. In this regard, a 1-technique defender who is aligned on an offensive tackle must read the high hat and explode upfield with his big first step. The pass-rushing defensive tackle should set up the inside move through the B gap—particularly when rushing from the 1-technique alignment over the offensive tackle. When rushing from either a 1-technique or 2-technique alignment over the offensive tackle, the defensive tackle normally has outside help from a teammate on an outside rush over the tight end. Furthermore, a defender who rushes from either a 1-technique or 2-technique alignment over the tackle is usually given more leverage to the inside. The inside leverage is a result of the accompanying nose tackle rushing to the side of the outside-technique defender on the opposite side. As a general rule, unless a stunt is called, the interior defensive lineman who is using his outside foot as an anchor should rush to the inside of the pass blocker.

The appropriate reactions of a 3-technique defensive lineman to an offensive tackle's pass block are basically the same as for both a 1-technique and 2-technique defender. For example, a pass-rushing 3-technique defender aligned on the offensive tackle must read the high hat and explode upfield with his big first step. In this regard, however, one important difference between the three types of defensive alignment techniques involves what position the defender plays. A pass-rushing 3-technique defensive tackle should set up the inside move through the B gap, while a pass-rushing 3-technique defensive end should set up the outside move. Diagrams 5-38 through

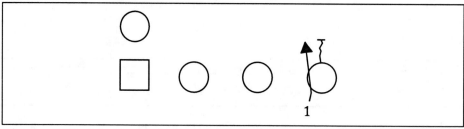

Diagram 5-38. A tackle dropback pass block versus a defensive end aligned in a 1 technique

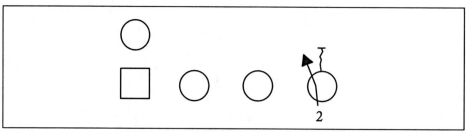

Diagram 5-39. A tackle dropback pass block versus a defensive end aligned in a 2 technique

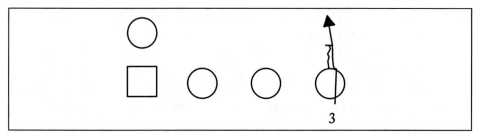

Diagram 5-40. A tackle dropback pass block versus a defensive end aligned in a 3 technique

5-40 show a defensive tackle in a 1, 2, and 3 technique, respectively, against a tackle's dropback pass block.

Guard Dropback Pass Block

Against a guard's pass block, a defensive lineman in either a 1 technique or 2 technique who is aligned over the offensive guard must react in essentially the same manner. For example, a defender who is aligned on an offensive guard must read the high hat and explode upfield with his big first step. The pass-rushing 1-technique or 2-technique defensive guard should set up the inside move through the A gap, particularly when rushing from an alignment over the offensive guard.

As the 1-technique or 2-technique defensive guard reads the high hat and throws his hands to the numbers of the offensive guard, he should also throw his eyes inside. By doing so, he readies himself to play an influence trap, which may be initiated with a fake pass block by the offensive guard. Inside alignment shades on the offensive guard are favorite prey for an influence trap. The pass-rushing 1-technique or 2-technique defender over an offensive guard must be trained to recognize an influence trap by the time the defensive lineman plants his second step upfield. If the defender on the offensive guard reads an influence trap, he should drop low to the ground and attack the trapper with his outside shoulder. When playing the influence trap, the defensive guard should try to keep his head up and his shoulders as square to the line of scrimmage as possible.

If the pass rusher reads the center to be setting for pass, he can be relatively certain that no threat of an influence trap exists. On the other hand, if a 1 technique or a 2 technique on the offensive guard reads a high hat on the center along with a high hat on the guard, the read is clearly a pass. Once he reads pass, the defender should execute one of the basic interior pass-rush techniques at his disposal, such as the rip, bull rush, or push-pull.

One coaching point that should be emphasized in this situation involves the fact that both 1-technique and 2-technique defensive linemen should be trained to be aware of the offensive lineman to their inside. A defender who attacks, but cannot read the offensive lineman to his inside, will often fall victim to influence traps. It is important to keep in mind that a successful influence trap will break down the integrity of any defensive-front scheme. As such, this factor also applies to the 1-technique or the 2-technique defender who aligns over either an offensive tackle or a tight end. In reality, all defenders aligned in either a 1 technique or a 2 technique are vulnerable to an influence trap.

Similar to the reactions required of a defender aligned in either a 1 or 2 technique against a guard dropback pass block, the 3-technique defensive guard must read the high hat and explode upfield with his big first step. Compared to the other two techniques, however, a pass-rushing 3-technique defensive guard has an alignment advantage in getting a big first step and using a rip technique to clear the blocker. Furthermore, a 3-technique defensive guard normally has the option of rushing to the inside or outside.

Like both the 1-technique and 2-technique defensive linemen, the 3-technique defender must be prepared to play an influence trap. If the 3-technique defender on the offensive guard reads an influence trap, he should drop low to the ground and attack with his outside shoulder. When playing an influence trap, the defensive 3-technique guard should try to keep his head up and his shoulders as square to the line of scrimmage as possible. Diagrams 5-41 through 5-43 illustrate how a defender

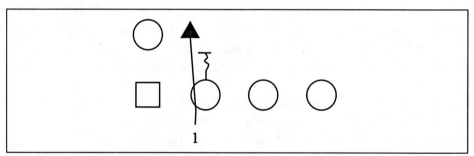

Diagram 5-41. A guard dropback pass block versus a defensive guard aligned in a 1 technique

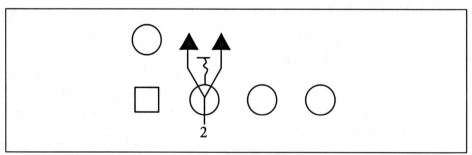

Diagram 5-42. A guard dropback pass block versus a defensive guard aligned in a 2 technique

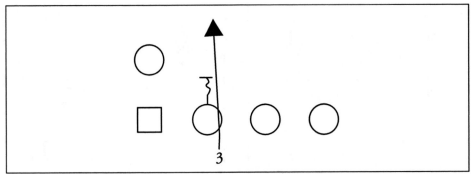

Diagram 5-43. A guard dropback pass block versus a defensive guard aligned in a 3 technique

aligned in a 1 technique, 2 technique, or 3 technique, respectively, should react to a guard dropback pass block.

Tight End Draw Block

Regardless of whether he is aligned in a 1, 2, or 3 technique, a defensive end has essentially the same reaction responsibilities when playing against a tight end draw block. After getting off on the ball with a big first step, the defensive end should close the distance to the tight end. Because the defender has a priority of gaining outside leverage against a pass-blocking tight end, he will get a slow read on the draw. Once the defensive end sees the draw, he should plant his outside foot to retrace his pass-rushing path from the line of scrimmage. The primary objective of the defensive end against the draw is to divert the path of the running back. A key coaching point that should be emphasized involves the fact that a defensive pass rusher must not stop to play a draw until he is sure that the ball was handed off. A defensive lineman must keep in mind that he should play the pass and react to the run. Diagrams 5-44 through 5-46 illustrate a tight end draw block against a defensive end aligned in a 1 technique, 2 technique, and 3 technique, respectively.

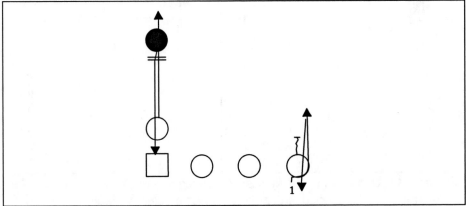

Diagram 5-44. A tight end draw block versus a defensive end aligned in a 1 technique

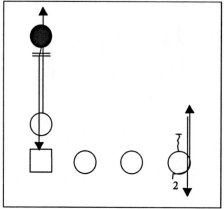

Diagram 5-45. A tight end draw block versus a defensive end aligned in a 2 technique

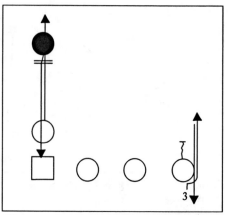

Diagram 5-46. A tight end draw block versus a defensive end aligned in a 3 technique

Tackle Draw Block

Against a tackle draw block, the reactions of a defensive tackle are essentially the same—regardless of whether he is aligned in a 1 technique, 2 technique, or 3 technique. In this situation, he should use a big first step to take off on the snap and throw his hands into the offensive tackle to get his hat in the crack of the B gap. Reading the high hat of the offensive tackle, the defender should then use his upper-body strength to lift the offensive tackle's shoulders and push the seam. Once the pass rusher recognizes that the ball has been handed off to the running back on a draw play, he should plant his feet, push off the pass protector to retrace his pass-rushing path, and restrict the hole for the running back. Diagrams 5-47 through 5-49 illustrate a tackle draw block against a defensive tackle aligned in a 1 technique, 2 technique, and 3 technique, respectively.

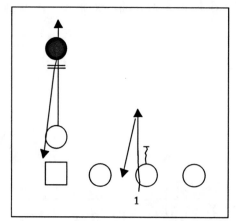

Diagram 5-47. A tackle draw block versus a defensive tackle aligned in a 1 technique

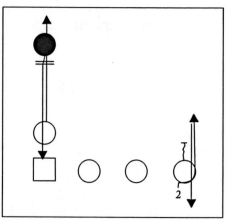

Diagram 5-48. A tackle draw block versus a defensive tackle aligned in a 2 technique

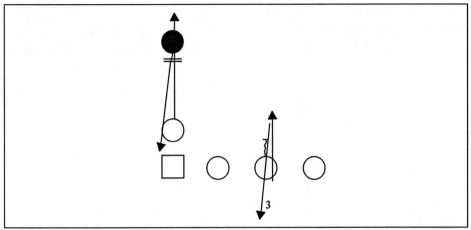

Diagram 5-49. A tackle draw block versus a defensive tackle aligned in a 3 technique

Guard Draw Block

As with a tackle draw block, the reactions of a defensive lineman against a guard draw block are essentially the same, regardless of whether the defender is aligned in a 1 technique, 2 technique, or 3 technique. For example, a defensive guard will usually face a combination block by the center. After getting off with the first big step and reading the offensive guard's high hat, a defensive tackle should use his upper-body strength to push the middle pass-rushing lane. In so doing, he can typically recognize a draw play through one of two reads. On one hand, he might read a draw by seeing the ball handed off to the running back. On the other hand, he might read a draw by feeling the center's release to the linebacker. On a draw play, the center will usually help to secure the closest defensive lineman, and then release to the linebacker after delaying to sell the draw. An experienced defensive tackle can normally recognize the center's action on a draw play. If the defensive tackle reads a draw, he should push off

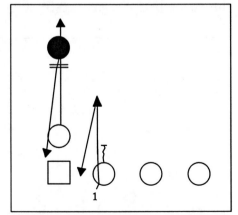

Diagram 5-50. A guard draw block versus a defensive guard aligned in a 1 technique

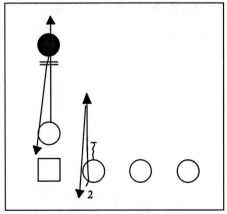

Diagram 5-51. A guard draw block versus a defensive guard aligned in a 2 technique

the guard, retrace his steps back to the line of scrimmage, and restrict the hole for the running back. Diagrams 5-50 through 5-52 illustrate a guard draw block against a defender aligned in a 1 technique, 2 technique, and 3 technique, respectively.

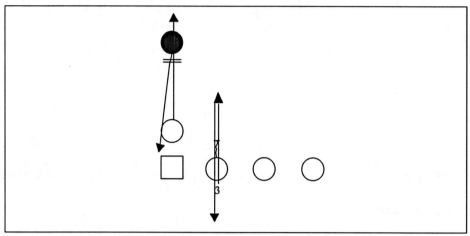

Diagram 5-52. A guard draw block versus a defensive guard aligned in a 3 technique

Tight End Dash Block

Essentially, the reactions of a defensive end aligned in a 1 technique, 2 technique, or 3 technique are quite similar. For example, the defensive end should attack the tight end with a big first step. He should locate the screws of the tight end's headgear as he explodes upfield. Because a tight end dash block resembles a hook block, a defensive end aligned in either a 1 technique or 2 technique should push through the inside shoulder of the tight end, while a 3-technique defensive end should push through the outside shoulder of the tight end. The major identifying feature of a dash block is the high hat of the tight end. As a result, what appears to the defender to be a hook block with a high hat is actually a dash block. In this situation, the defensive end should work to make a move on the tight end and sack the quarterback. Diagrams 5-53 through

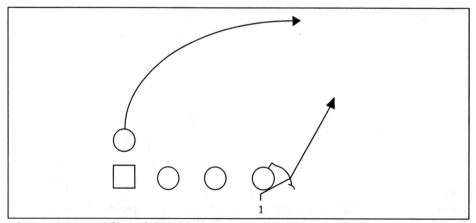

Diagram 5-53. A tight end dash block versus a defensive end aligned in a 1 technique

5-55 illustrate a tight end dash block against a defender aligned in a 1 technique, 2 technique, and 3 technique, respectively.

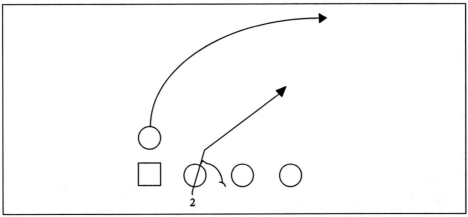

Diagram 5-54. A tight end dash block versus a defensive end aligned in a 2 technique

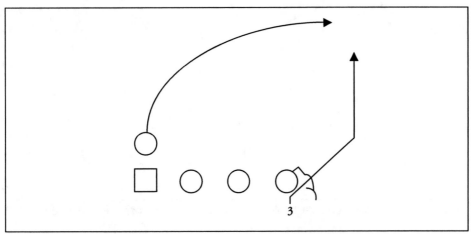

Diagram 5-55. A tight end dash block versus a defensive end aligned in a 3 technique

Tight End Dash Block Away

Aside from the fact that a 3-technique defensive end attacks to the outside of a tight end, while 1-technique and 2-technique defenders work to the inside, the reactions of a defensive end to a tight end dash block away are essentially the same. The defensive end takes off on the snap and reads the high hat set of the tight end and tackle. Using a big first step to gain closure, the defensive end aligned in either a 1 technique or 2 technique gets his hat in the C gap and attacks the inside half of the tight end. Both the 1-technique and 2-technique defensive ends then drive the inside pad through the outside shoulder of the offensive tackle in an effort to get around the edge of the offensive tackle's dash block set. The 3 technique, on the other hand, from a trailing position, uses a rip technique to get around the outside edge of the tight end. Regardless of the technique alignment used, the defensive end should react to any

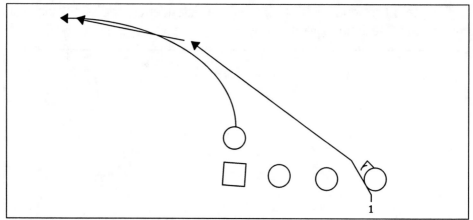

Diagram 5-56. A tight end dash block away versus a defensive end aligned in a 1 technique

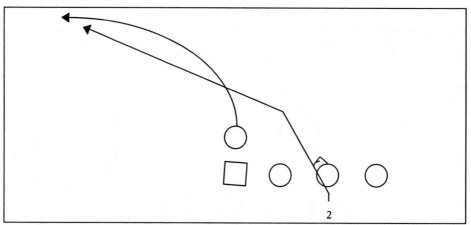

Diagram 5-57. A tight end dash block away versus a defensive end aligned in a 2 technique

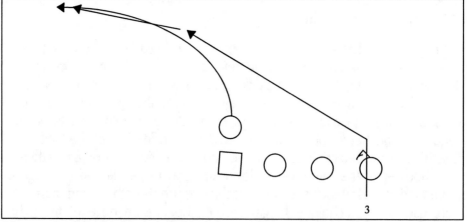

Diagram 5-58. A tight end dash block away versus a defensive end aligned in a 3 technique

flow across his face (e.g., a throwback screen) as he attempts to get around the blocker and pressure the quarterback. Diagrams 5-56 through 5-58 illustrate a tight end dash block away against a defender aligned in a 1 technique, 2 technique, and 3 technique, respectively.

Tackle Dash Block Away

With a few differences for the 3 technique, the reactions of a defensive tackle against a tackle dash block away are essentially the same, regardless of the technique being employed. For example, a defensive tackle should attack the line of scrimmage on the snap with a big first step. Both 1-technique and 2-technique defenders take notice of the inside blocker (the offensive guard) and read the high hat of the offensive guard. The 3 technique, on the other hand, reads the high hat of the offensive tackle. Among the factors that should be looked for in a high-hat read on a tackle dash block away are the offensive tackle sliding inside and the offensive guard popping his head up. The combination of the inside slide by the offensive tackle and the double high-hat read cues both the 1-technique and 2-technique defensive tackle to run through the B gap by driving his inside shoulder through the outside shoulder of the offensive guard. The 3-technique defensive tackle, on the other hand, makes an inside move if the B gap isn't sealed by the offensive tackle. If the B gap is sealed by the offensive tackle, the 3-technique defender drives his inside shoulder through the outside shoulder of the offensive tackle, gets upfield quickly, and turns the corner. Regardless of the technique alignment he employs, the pass rusher uses his hands to work a move on either the guard (1 technique or 2 technique) or the offensive tackle (3 technique) and to gain clearance and make a break to the quarterback. Diagrams 5-59 through 5-61 illustrate a tackle dash block away against a defender aligned in a 1 technique, 2 technique, and 3 technique, respectively.

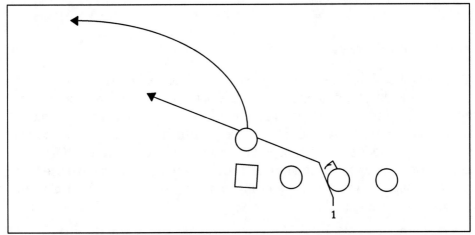

Diagram 5-59. A tackle dash block away versus a defensive end aligned in a 1 technique

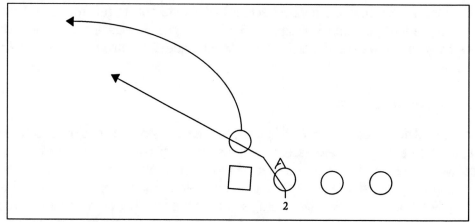

Diagram 5-60. A tackle dash block away versus a defensive end aligned in a 2 technique

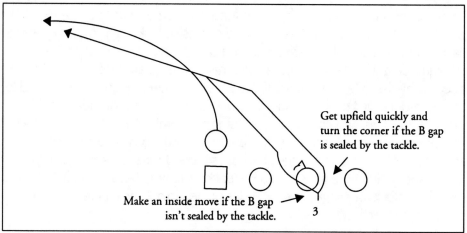

Get upfield quickly and turn the corner if the B gap is sealed by the tackle.

Make an inside move if the B gap isn't sealed by the tackle.

Diagram 5-61. A tackle dash block away versus a defensive end aligned in a 3 technique

Guard Dash Block Away

Against a guard dash block away, a defensive guard aligned in either a 1 technique or 2 technique should get off on the snap with a big step and read the combination of a high-hatted slide inside by the guard and a high-hat read of the inside blocker. In this instance, both a 1-technique and 2-technique pass rusher should continue to put their hats in the A-gap crack and run through the near shoulder of the center. With the inside shoulder driving through the center's near shoulder, the defender should use his hands to take advantage of any imbalance of the center's dash-block technique and gain a clear shot to the quarterback.

While both a 1 technique and 2 technique (as defenders who are responsible for the inside gap) will drive for the center's near shoulder, a 3-technique defender against a guard dash block will engage the outside shoulder of the offensive guard and attempt to round the short edge of the guard's pass set. Another strategic option for the 3 technique is for him to push upfield against the offensive guard's outside shoulder and quickly dip and rip across the face of the guard to penetrate the inside gap. In this instance, a 3-technique defender would engage the center in the same manner as a 1 technique or 2 technique. Diagrams 5-62 through 5-64 illustrate a guard dash block away against a defender aligned in a 1 technique, 2 technique, and 3 technique, respectively.

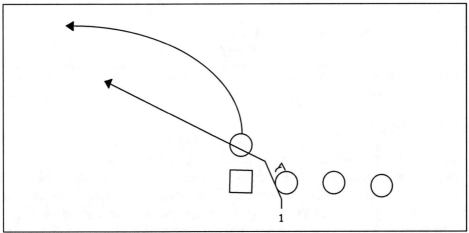

Diagram 5-62. A guard dash block away versus a defensive guard aligned in a 1 technique

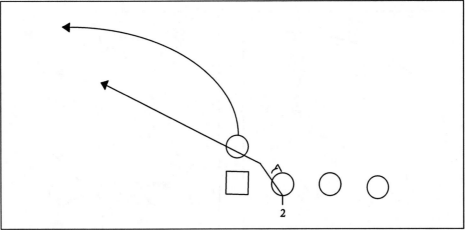

Diagram 5-63. A guard dash block away versus a defensive guard aligned in a 2 technique

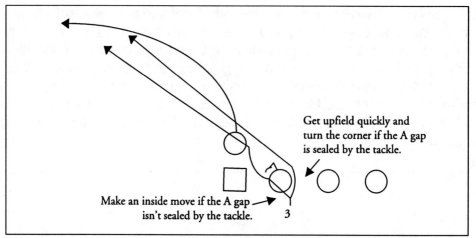

Get upfield quickly and turn the corner if the A gap is sealed by the tackle.

Make an inside move if the A gap isn't sealed by the tackle.

3

Diagram 5-64. A guard dash block away versus a defensive guard aligned in a 3 technique

Sprint Pass Block

An offensive blocker executes a sprint pass block or a hook block. As a consequence, the reactions and techniques that a defender should use to defeat the blocker and apply pressure on the quarterback depend on the method of sprint pass block used. Diagrams 5-65 through 5-67 illustrate a sprint pass block against a defender aligned in a 1 technique, 2 technique, and 3 technique, respectively. Diagrams 5-68 through 5-70, on the other hand, show a sprint pass block in which the blocker uses a hook block against a defensive lineman who is aligned in a 1 technique, 2 technique, and 3 technique, respectively.

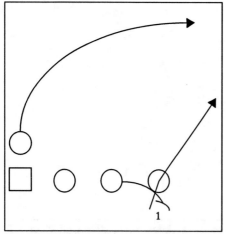

Diagram 5-65. A sprint pass block (reach method) versus a defensive end aligned in a 1 technique

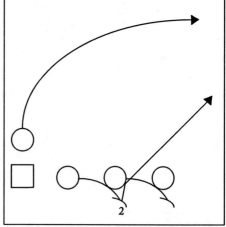

Diagram 5-66. A sprint pass block (reach method) versus a defensive end aligned in a 2 technique

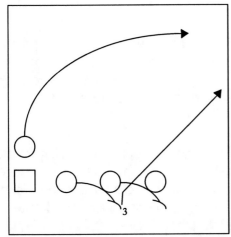

Diagram 5-67. A sprint pass block (reach method) versus a defensive end aligned in a 3 technique

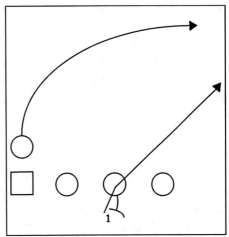

Diagram 5-68. A sprint pass block (hook method) versus a defensive end aligned in a 1 technique

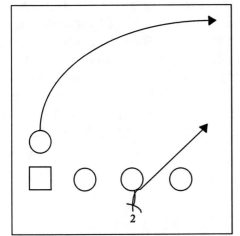

Diagram 5-69. A sprint pass block (hook method) versus a defensive end aligned in a 2 technique

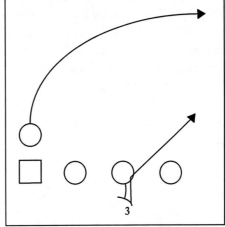

Diagram 5-70. A sprint pass block (reach method) versus a defensive end aligned in a 3 technique

Against a sprint pass block, a 3-technique defender attempts to maintain outside leverage and fight upfield to pressure a sprint-out passer. On the other hand, both a 1 technique and a 2 technique are placed at a significant disadvantage because of their alignment. As such, both the 1 technique and the 2 technique should take the least restrictive route to the quarterback. Accordingly, they should normally fight across the face of the blocker to get to the outside (whereas a 3 technique simply has to fight to maintain his alignment leverage). A coaching point that should be emphasized is that if the blocker overcommits, both the 1 technique and the 2 technique may slip underneath (i.e., behind) the sprint pass blocker to get into either the proper pursuit angle or the appropriate pass-rushing lane.

Fold Block

A fold block is an angle block on the first defensive lineman to the outside of the fold blocker. As a rule, a fold block is a block performed in conjunction with the block of the primary blocker, who is pulling either to the onside or the offside. Essentially, regardless of the alignment technique he employs, a defender responds to a fold block in a similar manner.

As such, the defender gets off on the ball and explodes upfield with a big first step. He gets his hat in the crack and reads the earhole of the primary blocker's headgear. Against a fold block from the inside, the defender should drop his inside shoulder and wheel backdoor to make the play. To wheel backdoor, the defender should flatten his path down the line of scrimmage behind the old block. Against a fold block from the outside, the defender should react the same way he does against a U block (i.e., drop his outside shoulder and wheel backdoor to the outside).

An important coaching point that should be emphasized is the fact that a 1 technique or 2 technique* should always be aware of the weight distribution of the primary blocker and the inside blocker when they are in their stances. If the primary blocker is light on his hands and the inside blocker is sitting "heavy" in his stance, a high probability of a fold block being attempted exists. A fold block by the center versus a defensive guard aligned in a 1 technique requires a quick step by the center into the defensive guard (Diagram 5-71). A fold block by the center versus a defensive guard aligned in a 2 technique requires a flatter step by the center (Diagram 5-72) A fold block

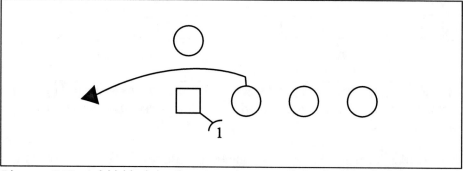

Diagram 5-71. A fold block by the center versus a defensive guard aligned in a 1 technique

*Because a 3 technique is an outside shade, he doesn't look through his primary blocker to the inside blocker to see the blocker tipping a fold block. Even more importantly, the blocker who is light on his hands (and, therefore, tipping off a fold block) would be the outside blocker in this situation—not the inside blocker. The offensive lineman that the 3 technique would be looking at would be the primary blocker. In a fold block, this individual would not be light on his hands. He would be firing out at full speed to drive the 3 technique outward, as the outside blocker folds underneath to the inside.

by the center versus a defensive guard aligned in a 3 technique requires a position step by the center, when then waits for the defender to react to him (Diagram 5-73).

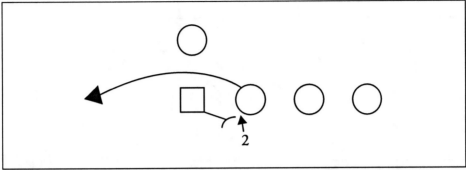

Diagram 5-72. A fold block by the center versus a defensive guard aligned in a 2 technique

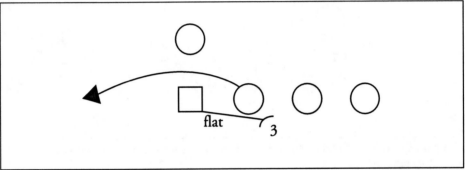

Diagram 5-73. A fold block by the center versus a defensive guard aligned in a 3 technique

Reach Block

On a reach block, the ball is moving toward the offside—away from the defender. With only a few differences, a reach block is played in exactly the same manner by each of the three types of technique alignments. On the snap of the ball, the defender drives off the ball with a big step and gets his hat in the crack. He then reads the screws of the primary blocker and gets an earhole read (i.e., the blocker turns his head so that the defender can see his earhole). In making such a read, a defender aligned in a 1 technique or 2 technique ricochets off the blocker on whom he is aligned (i.e., the primary blocker) and squeezes inside down the line of scrimmage. The 3 technique,* on the other hand, ricochets off the blocker to his outside (not the blocker on whom he is aligned). He then squeezes down the line of scrimmage. By flattening out to

*A 3-technique defensive end will never encounter a reach block unless a wing is aligned to his outside. In that scenario, the defender should play a reach block the same way a 3-technique defensive tackle or a 3-technique defensive guard would.

defeat the reach block, the defender is able to stay on his feet to effectively pursue the ballcarrier. Diagrams 5-74 through 5-76 illustrate a reach block against a defender aligned in a 1 technique, 2 technique, and 3 technique, respectively.

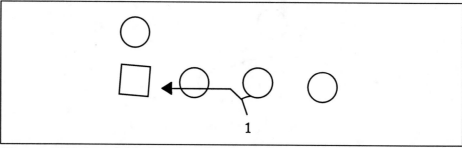

Diagram 5-74. A reach block by the offensive tackle versus a defensive guard aligned in a 1 technique

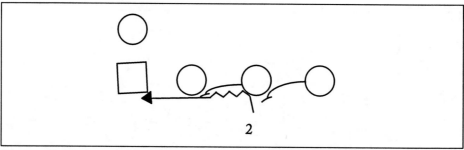

Diagram 5-75. A reach block by the offensive tackle versus a defensive guard aligned in a 2 technique

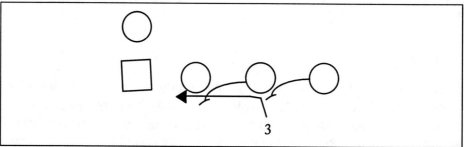

Diagram 5-76. A reach block by the offensive tackle versus a defensive guard aligned in a 3 technique

Reach Block From Cheated Splits

From cheated splits, a reach block is employed against both a 1 technique and a 2 technique. When the defender notices a cheated split (i.e., undersplit or foot-to-foot split), he realizes that a reach block is a likely possibility. Upon recognizing the cheated split between the blockers, the defender should tighten his alignment. A 1-technique defender tightens to a gap alignment, while a 2 technique assumes a 1-technique gap alignment.

The defender should explode upfield on the snap of the ball, but not with his customary big first step. Since the cheated split eliminates the possibility of a crack for the defensive player to get his hat into, he should shorten his initial step. His primary objective should be to grab the inside offensive lineman as the blocker attempts to reach inside. The defender should ricochet off of the reach blocker to the outside and flatten out to pursue inside. He should stay on his feet as he fights down the line of scrimmage in an attempt to make the hit on the ballcarrier.

A reach block from cheated splits is not applicable against a 3-technique defender, because a 3 technique will widen his alignment versus cheated splits (i.e., move outside to a 1-technique alignment on the next offensive lineman). Even if a 3 technique didn't widen his alignment, cheated side splits would not affect his reactions against a reach-block scheme. Diagrams 5-77 and 5-78 illustrate a reach block from cheated splits against a defender aligned in a 1 technique and 2 technique, respectively.

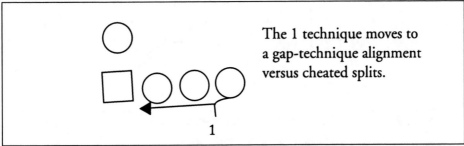

The 1 technique moves to a gap-technique alignment versus cheated splits.

Diagram 5-77. A reach block from cheated splits versus a defensive guard aligned in a 1 technique

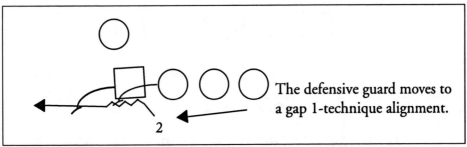

The defensive guard moves to a gap 1-technique alignment.

Diagram 5-78. A reach block from cheated splits versus a defensive guard aligned in a 2 technique

Scoop Block

On a scoop block, the ball is moving toward the onside (i.e., toward the defender). Similar to a reach block from cheated splits, a scoop block is not applicable against a 3-technique defender.

A 1 technique and 2 technique should play a scoop block in the same manner. On the snap of the ball, the defender should attack the line of scrimmage with a big first step and get his head in the crack. He then should ricochet to the outside off the scoop blocker and wheel backdoor. Next, he should flatten out his path to pursue the ballcarrier outside. It is important to note that a scoop is rarely employed against either a defensive tackle or a defensive end, unless it is used in combination with a rub technique by the primary blocker. In reality, a scoop block is most typically seen by a defensive guard.

A 3 technique is not scoop blocked, because his outside shade alignment makes it impossible—and unsound—for an inside blocker to be assigned to block him. As such, only a 1 technique or a 2 technique will encounter a scoop block by an inside blocker. Diagrams 5-79 and 5-80 illustrate a scoop block against a defender aligned in a 1 technique and 2 technique, respectively.

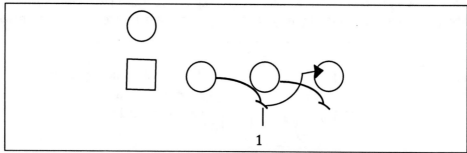

Diagram 5-79. A scoop block versus a defensive tackle aligned in a 1 technique

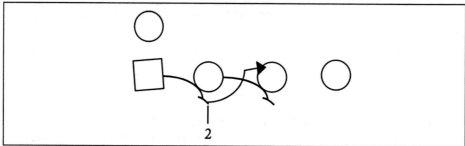

Diagram 5-80. A scoop block versus a defensive tackle aligned in a 2 technique

Technique Play Against Trap Blocks

Influence Trap

Essentially, a trap block is played in the same manner by a defensive lineman regardless of what technique alignment he assumes. As such, an influence trap is characterized by the primary blocker showing a high hat and inviting the defender to penetrate upfield. As the defender reads the high hat and throws his hands to the numbers of the primary blocker, the defender should shoot his eyes inside to ready himself to play against an influence trap. Although the inside alignment shades on the offensive guard are most often attacked with an influence trap, an outside alignment is also schemed with an influence trap. The pass rushing defensive guard must be trained to recognize an influence trap by the time he plants his second step upfield. If the defender reads an influence trap, he should drop low to the ground and attack the trapper with his outside shoulder. When playing against an influence trap, a defensive tackle should try to keep his head up and his shoulders as square to the line of scrimmage as possible. Defensive linemen should be trained not only to sacrifice their bodies to clog the inside gap, but also to pry through the trap block and make the tackle. Diagrams 5-81 through 5-83 illustrate an influence trap block against a defender aligned in a 1 technique, 2 technique, and 3 technique, respectively.

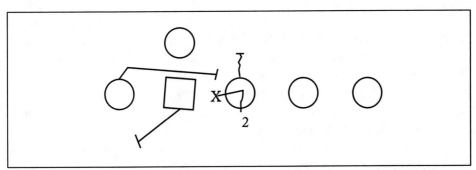

Diagram 5-81. An influence trap block versus a defensive end aligned in a 1 technique

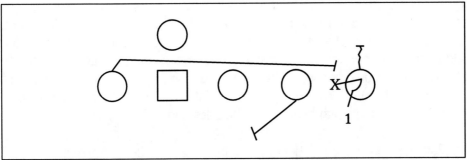

Diagram 5-82. An influence trap block versus a defensive guard aligned in a 2 technique

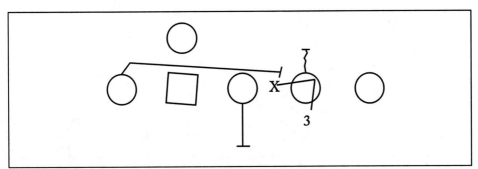

Diagram 5-83. An influence trap block versus a defensive tackle aligned in a 3 technique

Bluff Trap

A bluff trap block is specifically designed for a defender aligned in an inside shade, although it is relatively productive when used to attack a 3-technique defensive end or defensive tackle. Against a bluff trap, the major difference between the reactions of either a 1 technique or 2 technique and those of a 3 technique involves the type of read the defender uses.

The bluff trap gives both the 1 technique and the 2 technique a "grass read." In playing a bluff trap, the defender gets off on the snap of the ball and explodes upfield with a big first step. When the bluff trap develops, the defensive lineman is left in a gaping area as the inside blocker goes inside and the primary blocker blocks outside. As the running back attacks the 1-technique or 2-technique defender's outside shoulder, the defender finds himself standing unmolested in the grass (thus, a "grass read"). He should quickly shift his focus to the inside and pick up the angle of the trapping guard. If the offensive guard is on a flat angle toward him, he should attack the guard's inside knee with his outside shoulder and spill the play.

A bluff trap, on the other hand, gives the 3 technique a down-block read by a primary blocker. Whenever a 3-technique defensive lineman gets a down-block read, he should quickly shift his focus to the inside and pick up the angle of the trapping guard. If the offensive guard is on a flat angle toward him, he should attack the guard's inside knee with his outside shoulder and spill the play. The near back will attempt to attack the outside shoulder of the defensive lineman to "bluff" a log block. The aim of the bluff is to get the 3-technique defender to attack the running back and fight outside—thereby opening a gaping hole for the trapping linemen. Diagrams 5-84 through 5-86 illustrate a bluff trap against a defender aligned in a 1 technique, 2 technique, and 3 technique, respectively.

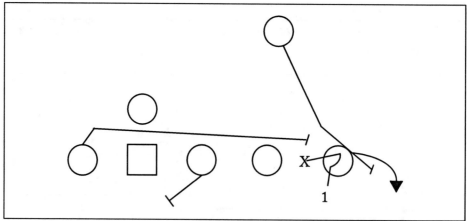

Diagram 5-84. A bluff trap block versus a defensive end aligned in a 1 technique

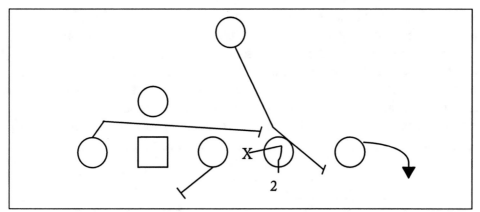

Diagram 5-85. A bluff trap block versus a defensive tackle aligned in a 2 technique

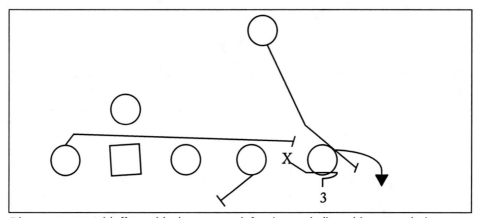

Diagram 5-86. A bluff trap block versus a defensive end aligned in a 3 technique

Counter O-T Block

To stop the playside counter O-T block, a defensive lineman aligned in either a 1 technique or 2 technique should get off the snap of the ball and explode upfield with a big first step. He should use his outside shoulder to drive through the inside pad of the down blocker and penetrate by getting his head in the gap. Since the inside blocker is also blocking down on a playside counter O-T, the defensive lineman should be able to see the backside pulling linemen coming his way. He should attempt to force a bubble in the line of scrimmage and, ideally, knock the blocker off his path. A counter O-T block is most often employed against a defensive tackle, either from his inside shade alignment over the offensive tackle or offensive guard. The 1-technique or 2-technique defensive end will normally get an influence trap read by the tight end.

For the 3 technique, the counter O-T develops off of a down-block read. To stop the playside counter O-T, a 3 technique should throw his hands into the primary blocker to flatten the blocker's path. The defensive 3 technique should then use his inside shoulder to drive through the outside pad of the down blocker. He should bench press the blocker to the inside and turn the blocker's shoulders to keep him off his defensive teammate to the inside. The 3-technique defensive lineman should keep his pads low as he squeezes inside. As he squeezes inside, he should look through the hip of the down blocker and find the backside pulling lineman coming his way. The defensive lineman should then break off his squeeze and attack the pulling lineman's inside knee. By attacking the blocker's inside knee with his outside shoulder pad, the defender forces a bubble in the line of scrimmage and knocks the blocker off his path.

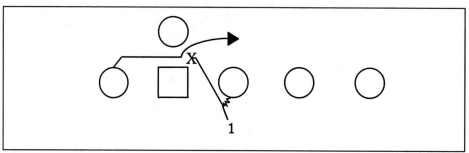

Diagram 5-87. A playside counter O-T block versus a defensive guard aligned in a 1 technique

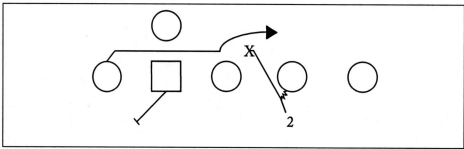

Diagram 5-88. A playside counter O-T block versus a defensive tackle aligned in a 2 technique

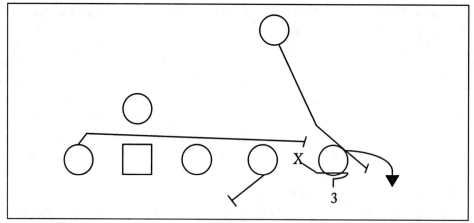

Diagram 5-89. A playside counter O-T block versus a defensive end aligned in a 3 technique

Diagrams 5-87 through 5-89 illustrate a counter O-T block against a defender aligned in a 1 technique, 2 technique, and 3 technique, respectively.

Bill-O

A Bill-O block is a spin-off (i.e., complementary type of play) of the bluff trap combination block. Regardless of his technique alignment, the reactions of the defender against a Bill-O block are essentially the same. From a defender's perspective, the Bill-O and the bluff trap are identical in appearance during the initial hat-in-the-crack phase of the attack. The key to recognizing the difference between the two types of blocks and defeating the Bill-O block is correctly reading the angle of the offensive guard. The guard's angle on a bluff trap is a flat trapping angle, while the guard's angle on the Bill-O is a deeper log angle. Instead of the near back bluffing the hook block as he does on the bluff trap, the Bill-O block is a combination block normally seen only by the defensive end and the defensive tackle, who is aligned on the offensive line.

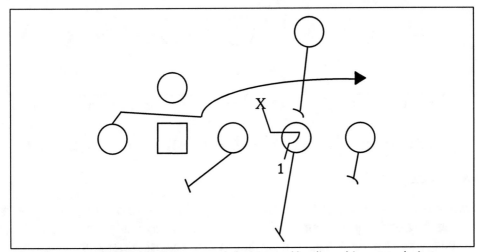

Diagram 5-90. A Bill-O block versus a defensive tackle aligned in a 1 technique

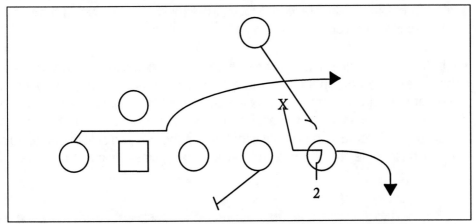

Diagram 5-91. A Bill-O block versus a defensive end aligned in a 2 technique

Against the Bill-O, the primary objective of the defender should be to work upfield and force the pulling guard to bubble around the wreck. The defender should keep his hands low to protect himself against the cut block from the offensive back. Diagrams 5-90 through 5-92 illustrate a Bill-O block against a defender aligned in a 1 technique, 2 technique, and 3 technique, respectively.

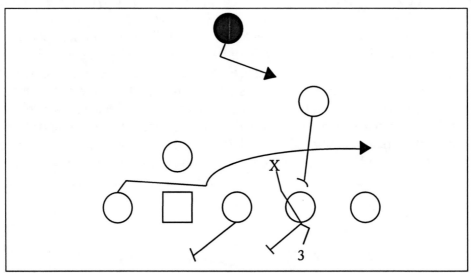

Diagram 5-92. A playside Bill-O block versus a defensive end aligned in a 3 technique

Technique Play Against a Combination Block

Power Block

A power block* is an inside-out double-team block that is employed against either a 1-technique or 2-technique defender. Because a power block is an inside-out double-team, this type of block would not be attempted against a defender in an outside shade alignment (i.e., a 3 technique). In this instance, a 3 technique will only encounter an outside-in double-team block (what most coaches would refer to as a pure double-team, or a combination block).

For both a 1 technique and 2 technique, the key to defeating a power block is to have the defender get off on the ball and get his hat in the crack. The primary aim of the defender should be to create a substantial "wreck" in the gaps as he penetrates the gap. The defender should dig in against a power block (as opposed to attempting to drop or spin out). As such, he should fight through the gap and split the power block. It is important to note that a power block is used against all three defensive line

*Note: Some coaches give specific names to an inside-out double-team block versus the more typical outside-in double-team block. A "power block" is an example of such an instance.

positions (i.e., guard, tackle, and end). Diagrams 5-93 through 5-95 illustrate a power block against a defensive guard, a defensive tackle, and a defensive end, respectively.

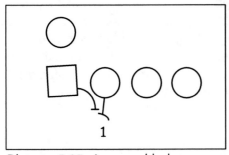

Diagram 5-93. A power block versus a defensive guard aligned in a 1 technique

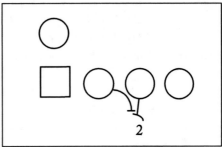

Diagram 5-94. A power block versus a defensive tackle aligned in a 2 technique

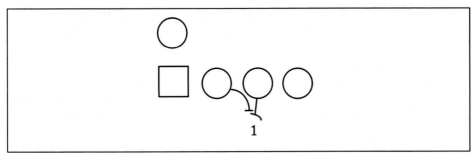

Diagram 5-95. A power block versus a defensive end aligned in a 1 technique

Double-Team Block

The double-team block consists of two blocks—a post block and a lead block. In reality, a post block is a drive block. On a post block, the primary blocker attempts to strike the defensive lineman underneath his chin and lift him. A lead block is the outside half of the double-team block. The lead blocker executes his block by pushing off his outside foot and taking a 45-degree slide step to the inside. The lead blocker attempts to keep his shoulders square and roll the defender backward to cut off the linebacker's pursuit.

A double-team block is employed against a 3-technique defender. Similar to the fact that a 3 technique doesn't see an inside-out double-team block, neither a 1 technique nor a 2 technique would encounter an outside-in double-team block. Remember, 1-technique and 2-technique defenders would face a power block combination, rather than a pure double-team or combination block. As such, it would be relatively foolhardy for a team to employ a scheme in which two blockers were sent from the outside on an inside shaded defender who is already outflanked by just one of the blockers.

Similar to a power block, one of the primary keys to defeating a double-team is to have the defender get off on the ball and get his hat in the crack. The aim of the

3-technique defender should be to create a major wreck as he penetrates the gap. Rather than attempt to drop or spin out, the defender should dig against the double-team block. He should fight through the gap and split the double-team block. The defender should be taught to hook his outside arm inside the knee of the lead blocker and take him down. Another key to defeating a double-team block is to beat the post blocker. In reality, a double-team block cannot normally be beaten if the primary blocker (i.e., the post blocker) achieves his intended movement. Diagrams 5-96 through 5-98 illustrate a double-team block against a defensive guard, a defensive tackle, and a defensive end, respectively.

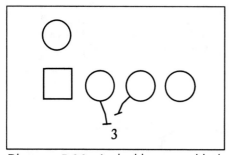

Diagram 5-96. A double team block versus a defensive guard aligned in a 3 technique

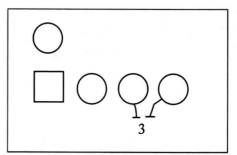

Diagram 5-97. A double team block versus a defensive tackle aligned in a 3 technique

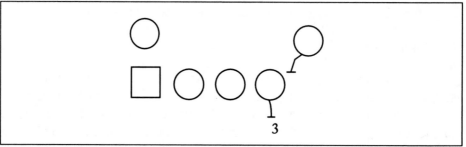

Diagram 5-98. A double team block versus a defensive end aligned in a 3 technique

U Block

A U block is a double-down combination block in which the outside blocker signals his blocking partner regarding which of the two of them should take on the inside defender (i.e., a call of "you" signals the partner to block the inside defender, while a call of "me" tells the partner that the outside blocker will take on the inside defender). All three types of technique alignments respond to a U block in essentially the same manner.

As a rule, a U block is only employed against a defensive guard or a defensive tackle. All factors considered, it is a relatively easy read because the inside blocker pulls to the outside across the defender's face. When the defender recognizes the blocker's pulling action, the defensive player should push off his inside foot and wheel backdoor.

If the down block of the primary blocker seals off the inside gap and the defender is captured, the defender should spin out or club the blocker with his outside arm and rip his inside arm across the blocker's face. Once the defender spins or clubs the blockers to clear the area, he should pursue flat down the line of scrimmage to the outside. Diagrams 5-99 through 5-101 illustrate a U block against a 1 technique, 2 technique, and 3 technique, respectively.

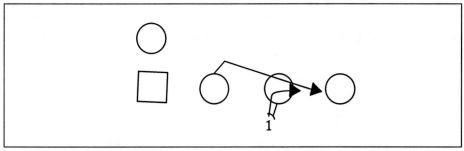

Diagram 5-99. A U block versus a defensive tackle aligned in a 1 technique

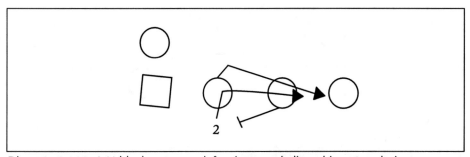

Diagram 5-100. A U block versus a defensive guard aligned in a 2 technique

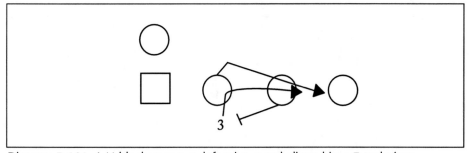

Diagram 5-101. A U block versus a defensive guard aligned in a 3 technique

Seal Block With an Offside Pull

A seal block with an outside pull is a combination block that is employed against a defensive end. Except for a few minor differences, the reactions of a defender are essentially the same against this type of block, regardless of his basic technique alignment. Even though the primary objective of a seal block is to seal the defender inside, the defender must get his hat in the crack and penetrate the C gap. The defender should maintain an appropriate relationship to the ballcarrier. The defensive end's responsibility is the C gap. It is important that the defensive end is fully aware of the fact that he must not abandon the C gap and charge upfield to defeat the blocker and leave the C gap open for the ballcarrier. By the same token, the 3-technique defender cannot afford to skate upfield and create a large crease in the C gap. Diagrams 5-102 and 5-103 show a seal block with an offside pull against a 1-technique and 2-technique defender, respectively. Diagram 5-104 shows a seal block against a 3-technique defender who is facing a very different type of situation. In Diagram 5-104, the ball is still inside. In this situation, the 3-technique defensive end is normally taught to not allow a crease to develop.

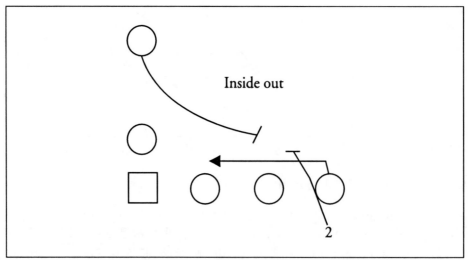

Diagram 5-102. A seal block with an offside pull versus a defensive end aligned in a 1 technique

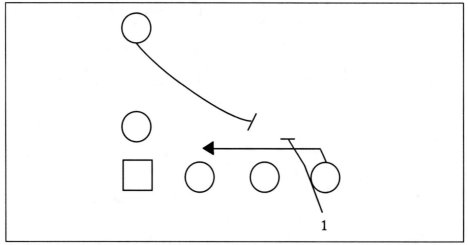

Diagram 5-103. A seal block with an offside pull versus a defensive end aligned in a 2 technique

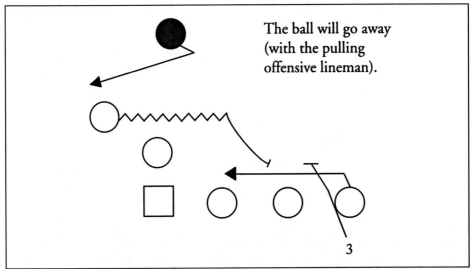

The ball will go away (with the pulling offensive lineman).

3

Diagram 5-104. A seal block with an offside pull versus a defensive end aligned in a 3 technique who is encountering a situation in which the ball is still inside

Zone Block

A zone block is an extremely common combination blocking scheme that is employed against a defender in all three basic technique alignments. A defender aligned in either a 1 technique or a 2 technique reacts to a zone block in essentially the same manner, while the responses of a 3-technique defender differ from the other two.

A defender in either a 1-technique or 2-technique alignment should get off on the ball to get his head in the crack. As he makes his second step, he should shorten his stride and rip upward with his backside arm (i.e., the arm nearest the primary blocker). The defender should then grab the inside blocker with his hands and ride him down to the inside. This action pulls the defender away from the primary blocker and helps him to flatten down the line of scrimmage (play the stretch of the offensive linemen). As such, the defender can use the primary blocker's momentum to help him push into the play as he rides the inside blocker. The defender should continue to work to the point of attack.

A 3-technique defender, on the other hand, has an entirely different perspective from his angle on a zone block—an outside-in view versus an inside-out view. Against a zone block away, the 3 technique should look inside, squeeze the line of scrimmage, and respond to either the traps or the lateral play by continuing to work against the point of attack. Against a zone block toward him, the 3 technique should occupy the onside gap and play the stretch to the point of attack. Diagrams 5-105 and 5-106 illustrate a zone block against a defensive tackle aligned in a 1 technique and 2 technique, respectively, while Diagram 5-107 shows a zone block against a defensive end.

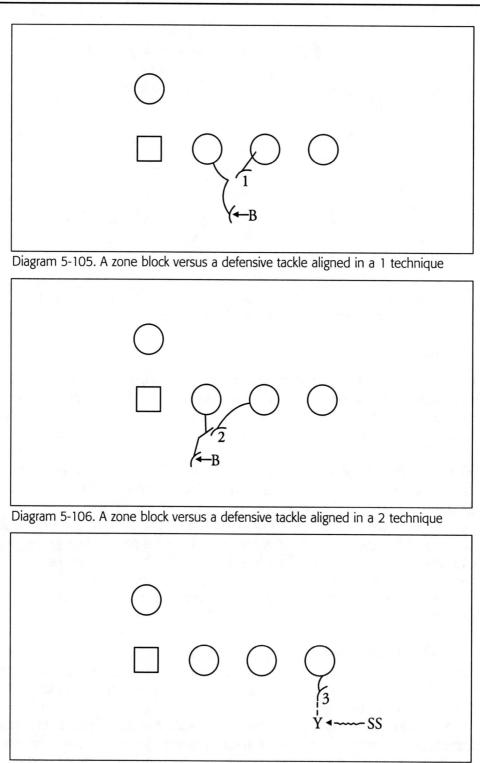

Diagram 5-105. A zone block versus a defensive tackle aligned in a 1 technique

Diagram 5-106. A zone block versus a defensive tackle aligned in a 2 technique

Diagram 5-107. A zone block versus a 3 technique defensive end

6

Stunts to Stop the Run and Pass

Defensive line games—particularly those geared toward providing a pass rush—are best when used as a change-up and as an additional factor to create a great jet pass-rush technique. It is the responsibility of the defensive line coach to develop stunts that take advantage of offensive schemes and individual player technique weaknesses demonstrated by the opponent. One of the primary keys to unlocking the code to recognizing and exploiting these weaknesses involves intensive film study and practice separation. An excellent approach for teaching and implementing effective stunts involves the following steps:

- *Talk it*—The purpose of the stunt, the key coaching points of the stunt, and the contingencies that may affect the execution of the stunt should be explained to the players during a chalk talk.
- *Walk it*—The aforementioned considerations should be more thoroughly discussed and explained during a walkthrough on the field, using defensive linemen to simulate the pass blockers.
- *Teach speed*—The stunts should be performed (practiced) in a slow, controlled manner under the direction of the defensive line coach, with primary emphasis on the major coaching points attendant to the stunt. Defensive linemen should be used to simulate pass blockers.

- *Practice speed*—The stunts should be run at a faster pace against offensive linemen who demonstrate a predetermined, specific pass-protection scheme. At this point, the emphasis should be placed on the sharpness of the execution of the particular stunting technique.

When deciding what stunt packages should be included in his team's defensive scheme, a defensive line coach should consider three questions:

- How many stunts does the team need? Stunts should never be included in a team's defensive scheme just for the sake of having stunts. Each stunt should have a specific purpose and address a specific need. Generally speaking, the number of stunts that are needed is related to two factors:
  - ✓ How good—or bad—is the team's base defensive production against the run or pass?
  - ✓ Is there a specific characteristic of the opponent's blocking that can be better attacked through a stunt?
- How much emphasis within the game plan should be placed on stunts? Again, the emphasis on stunts is usually related to the match-up of the team's opponent versus the defensive unit. A mismatch usually indicates that stunts should be a part of a team's defensive package. The irony of this consideration is that a mismatch can be either in a team's favor or in its opponent's favor. Certainly, whenever a team's opponent seriously outmatches it in size, strength, and ability, the defensive coach should consider an extensive stunt package. However, a stunt package is even more likely to be devastating to an opponent who is overmatched by a team's defensive personnel. Additional considerations that should be addressed when deciding how much emphasis should be placed on a stunt package within a team's weekly game plan are the element of surprise and the nature of the opponent's offensive system. In the National Football League, some teams pass more than others, while some run more than others. Nevertheless, if a defensive coach is able to inject an element of surprise into the game by tailoring his team's system to meet a specific attack, the emphasis on the stunt package should probably be increased for that week.
- How much variation is needed within a defensive stunt package? The number of stunts and the relative emphasis on the teaching of the various stunt combinations is directly related to a coach's decision regarding the amount of variation needed within the team's defensive stunt package. Generally speaking, the offensive system that a team is facing should also be a primary consideration in the makeup of a defensive team's stunt package. For example, an offensive team that utilizes a wide range of formation concepts dictates that the nature of a team's stunt package be relatively limited. Against such an offense, the stunt package should be confined to stunts that allow the call to be run without checking off. Including multiple check-offs and automatics in a team's defensive system will greatly undermine the aggressiveness of a team's defensive unit.

The Best Run Stunt in Football

All factors considered, the best run stunt is, without a doubt, the E-T stunt illustrated in Diagram 6-1. The E-T stunt consists of the defensive end penetrating through the B gap. Proper penetration by the defensive end is the key to the success of this particular stunt. Without sufficient penetration by the defensive end, this stunt will fail. When executing this stunt, the defensive end must take a short step up and in with his inside foot and then push off his outside foot and dip his outside pad as he rips his outside arm underneath the primary blocker. If aligned on the offensive tackle, the defensive end cannot allow the tackle to stop his penetration. Just as importantly, the defensive end cannot allow the guard to stop his penetration with a reach block.

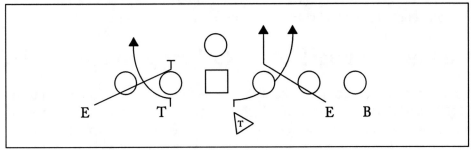

Diagram 6-1. An E-T stunt (shown to both sides)

The defensive tackle technique in an E-T stunt involves a slightly different takeoff than the big first step he normally uses. In an E-T stunt, the defensive tackle reads, then reacts. By reading the blocking pattern to determine the flow of the ball, a defensive tackle is able to either complete his part of the stunt or play off the blocker and get to

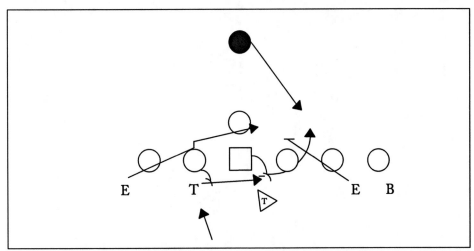

Diagram 6-2. An E-T stunt called to both sides. The defensive tackle doesn't finish the stunt, because the flow went to the opposite side. He should key the offensive guard's helmet. He should cut off the defensive end's buttocks—as opposed to looping around him.

the ball. Sending the defensive tackle on the stunt as a sell-out technique without regard for the flow of the ball diminishes the productivity of the stunt. The tackle will be wasted if the ball goes away from him. The reading technique of the defensive tackle before completing the stunt is called the "read-loop" technique. Diagram 6-2 illustrates a read-loop technique. The defensive tackle should continue on his stunt if his read shows pass. The defensive tackle should not loop until the defensive end gets into the gap.

This type of stunt can also be run by a defensive end and a tilted nose guard. A key coaching point for both the nose guard and the defensive tackle is the technique that is used by the defensive linemen to get through the C gap. When running this stunt, the nose guard or tackle must brush his inside shoulder to the buttocks of the penetrating end, ensuring a tight fit as he loops around the end.

The Best Dropback Pass-Rushing Stunt in Football

A strong argument can be made that the best pass-rushing stunt in football is the T-E stunt (Diagram 6-3). This stunt is highly dependent upon the threat of an effective jet-technique rush by the defensive end. Once the speed rush is established from a jet alignment, the offensive tackle is forced to focus on stopping the upfield charge of the defensive end. The T-E stunt begins with the defensive tackle penetrating through the outside gap (e.g., the B gap from the standard 4-3 alignment). As with the E-T stunt, adequate penetration is a must. If the defensive tackle is stopped from penetrating, the stunt will normally fail.

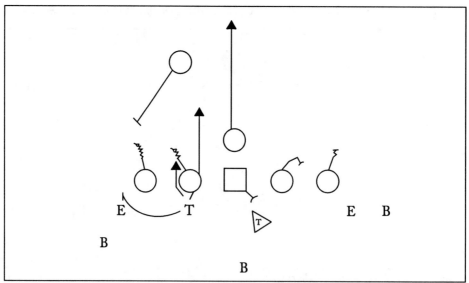

Diagram 6-3. A T-E stunt

A defensive tackle is able to gain penetration by using his outside hand to grab or slap the triceps of the offensive guard's arm. The defensive tackle should initiate his initial move on the snap of the ball; he cannot afford to make a head fake before grabbing the arm of the guard. He should violently pull (i.e., jerk the blocker's arm and shoulder downward and to the inside), and then use his inside arm to rip underneath and across the blocker's face. Once the defensive tackle gets his hat in the crack, the battle is essentially won. The defensive tackle's penetration pulls the offensive guard outward as he slides to pick up the defensive tackle. This action opens a crease for the defensive end to loop underneath. A defensive coach should assist the defensive tackle in accomplishing his objective by allowing him to operate from a shadow 3-technique alignment. The point to keep in mind is that a defensive line coach should place his defensive lineman in the alignment that will enable him to best accomplish his primary objective.

A defensive lineman should never be asked to stunt through an outside gap from a 1-technique alignment. Even a 2-technique alignment is not conducive to achieving penetration in an outside gap. Once a defensive tackle gets his hat in the crack and the defensive end begins his loop move, the tackle has containment. If the tackle breaks free, he will likely get the sack. When he breaks free, he should rush to the passing shoulder landmark of the quarterback.

The defensive end should sell the speed rush before looping underneath the defensive tackle's penetration. Selling the offensive tackle on the speed rush should make him push outside and back to pick up the jetting defensive end. This action helps to open the B gap wider for the penetrating defensive tackle. The defensive end should plant his outside foot to loop underneath as soon as he sees the defensive tackle gain penetration in the inside gap. Once the defensive tackle gets his hat in the crack, the defensive end should plant on his outside foot and drive underneath the defensive tackle. The defensive end should brush tightly to the buttocks of the defensive tackle as he loops up to gain clearance past the offensive guard.

A running back assigned to block the defensive end creates the mismatch that is the preferred match-up if a defensive stunt must be run against a three-on-two blocker-to-rusher ratio (Diagram 6-4). If possible, the T-E stunt should not be run to the side to which the center turns to help. A defensive line coach can help minimize the likelihood of a less-than-desirable three-on-two rusher-to-blocker group involving the center-guard-tackle against two pass rushers by studying his opponent's offensive formation tendencies and by determining the side to which the center will likely help in a zone or a man-protection scheme. By running the defensive stunt opposite the center (Diagram 6-5), the three-on-two blocker-to-rusher ratio can be limited to the less-advantageous running back-tackle-guard makeup.

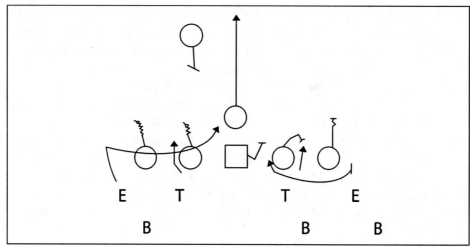

Diagram 6-4. A T-E stunt run to the 3-on-2 advantage on the center's helpside

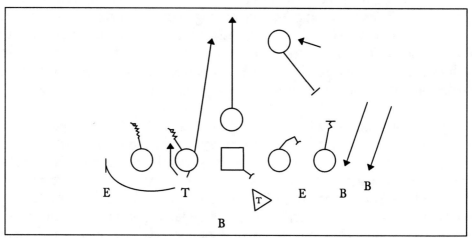

Diagram 6-5. A T-E stunt away from the center's set

The Best Stunt Versus Turnback Protection

Turnback protection is usually extremely effective against a four-man rush. As a rule, one very productive read stunt against turnback protection is a delayed loop through the backside A gap by the frontside defensive tackle. This type of stunt is most effective when run from an Eagle front or the "46" front. By running a tight loop behind the turnback protection of the center, the playside defensive tackle can get around the blockers to pressure the quarterback from behind. Diagram 6-6 shows a read loop stunt against the playside turnback protection. If the backside defensive tackle or the nose guard occupies the offensive center, the backside A gap should open up for the looping defensive tackle. In this situation, the playside offensive tackle who strictly adheres to his turnback protection rule of blocking the inside gap will be wasted, as he will have nobody to attack.

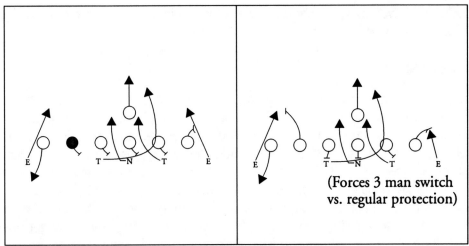

Diagram 6-6. Stunting against a turnback block

Two-Man Stunts

Two other examples of two-man defensive stunts are the Tom wide stunt and the Tom nose stunt:

Tom Wide Stunt

The defender designated as #1 in Diagram 6-7 gets off on the snap of the ball and gains ground (staying low and charging hard) with his near foot. He should step and rip in the A gap—low and hard. As he works upfield, he should push through the A gap to knock off the center. Defender #2 (the nose guard) should jab at the center to the bubble side (the nose guard's right). After jabbing, the nose guard should break toward defender #1. The nose guard should then loop tightly off the defensive tackle's

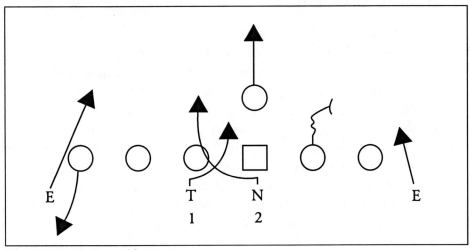

Diagram 6-7. A Tom wide stunt

buttocks and lower his inside shoulder, while looking in the area of the opposite guard to try to step around behind the penetration of the defensive tackle.

Tom Nose Stunt

In this stunt, defender #1 (the nose guard) should get off on the snap and gain ground (low and hard) with his foot nearest the center (Diagram 6-8). The nose guard should penetrate using a swim or a rip move. Turning his shoulders to make himself small, he should focus on the center. If the center slides away, the nose guard should ricochet off his back to get upfield. If the center blocks toward him, the nose guard should push a point through the line of scrimmage. Simultaneously, defender #2 should get off on the snap and fake an upfield charge. He should then loop tightly off the buttocks of the nose guard. He should then drive through the shoulder of the guard and get upfield. The defender can spin out to the offside if he feels himself not getting penetration.

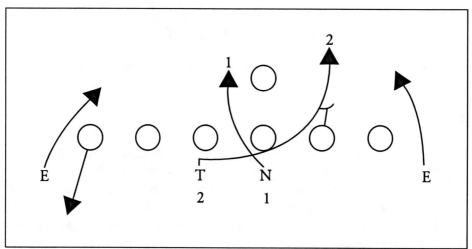

Diagram 6-8. A Tom nose stunt

The combining of the E-T and T-E stunts creates an excellent pass-rush combination called a mix stunt, which can be very successful (Diagram 6-9):
- The center usually slides or protects away from the running back. Therefore, defensive coaches can game-plan this stunt to use the E-T on the side of the center's blocking assignment and the T-E away from him.
- All linemen must be alert for the extra blocker, once they have defeated the offensive linemen. The center sliding should not be much of a problem for the E-T, since he really has no one to block. In addition, the T-E versus the guard and tackle is as good as it gets. Defensive linemen should drill the act of taking on the extra blocker when they get free from the offensive line.

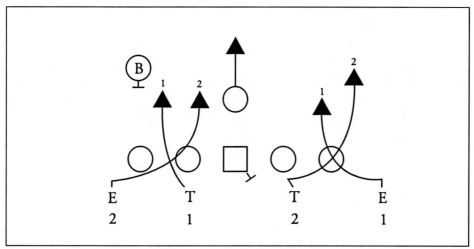

Diagram 6-9. Mix stunt

Three-Man Stunts

Tackle Around

This stunt is an excellent option versus a dropback pass, because the offensive right tackle is thinking E-T and is ready to switch, but doesn't get an early call from the right guard (Diagram 6-10). He therefore stays on the defensive end and the corner shortens for the tackle coming around. If the switch call occurs at that time, the defensive end is usually set free to the quarterback. The technique of the defensive end is the same as an E-T stunt. The tackle going inside must eventually try to cross the center's face. The tackle looping outside must contain the quarterback.

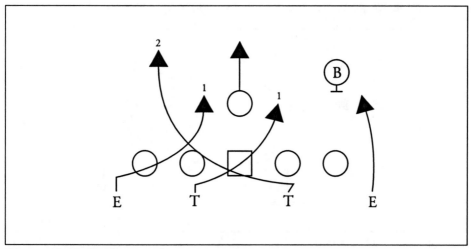

Diagram 6-10. Tackle around stunt

End Under

This stunt is an excellent three-man pass-rush stunt versus a dropback pass (Diagram 6-11). The right guard is thinking T-E stunt, but as he tries to switch, the other defensive tackle (he can align shaded on the center) is getting to the gap between him and the center, allowing the defensive end coming under to find a seam to the quarterback. The tackle starting the stunt must bounce outside to contain the quarterback.

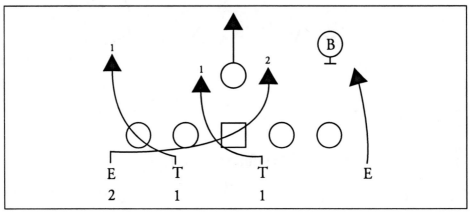

Diagram 6-11. End under stunt

Four-Man Stunt—Detroit

This stunt starts with the ends doing an E-T charge on both sides (Diagram 6-12). The difference occurs when the opposite tackle comes around the end for containment. He can cheat to a nose-shade alignment if necessary. The second tackle hesitates and then goes behind the first tackle to contain. Any one of the four linemen can come free. The right tackle goes first against a right-handed quarterback.

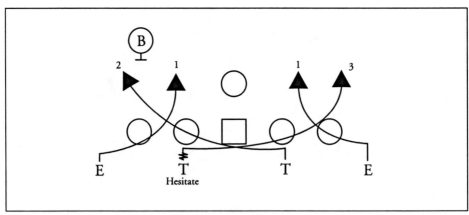

Diagram 6-12. Detroit stunt

7

Defensive Line Drills

One of the key features of a good defensive line drill is the game application that is achieved when the drill is performed during practice. As a rule, drills that have no real value in training an athlete to respond to game situations should be avoided. To be effective, a drill should meet at least the following criteria:

• *A drill should target one specific objective.*

Using a drill to develop multiple skills does not enable an athlete to focus on a particular target objective. Although a drill may involve multiple skills, it should have only one target objective. Additional skills that the athlete should possess to successfully engage in the drill should not only be skills that the athlete has already exhibited, but also has mastered to a degree.

• *A drill should be structured with the athlete's safety in mind.*

Coaches should never include activities in a drill that result in a player being injured. Drills that lead to injuries typically violate the principal of focusing on a singular objective. Coaches should keep in mind that athletes who are asked to perform drills that involve multiple tasks with which they are relatively unfamiliar face a higher risk of being injured during the finishing stage of such drills.

• *If possible, all defensive line drills should be started on ball movement—as opposed to starting on a cadence—unless two or three blockers are involved in a drill, in which case they can go on the first sound to get in as many repetitions as possible.*

Don't waste time during a drill with long, drawn out cadences. One illustration of a "bad" drill might involve an activity in which the players are asked to execute a series of complex (footwork) movements through an obstacle course of dummies positioned on the ground. As each player clears the final dummy, a coach then gives a hand signal to command the athlete to perform a two-point shoulder roll on the ground.

This drill has at least three design flaws, any of which could result in the athlete injuring his shoulder. First, an athlete should never be asked to perform a shoulder roll or other tumbling maneuver without the ground being padded. Second, an athlete should not be asked to perform a relatively risky activity (such as a two-point shoulder roll) on a last-second visual cue. The third flaw involves the game-situation relevancy of a shoulder roll. When does a situation arise where a football player has to execute a shoulder roll during a game? The answer is seldom—if ever. While a defensive player certainly needs to practice running over obstacles, the value of practicing shoulder rolls is dubious at best. Accordingly, a drill that involves two-point shoulder rolls appears to be not only needlessly hazardous to the athlete, but also poorly conceived.

• *A drill should develop a skill relevant to a player's position technique.*

Drills that develop skills and techniques that are rarely used—or are not part of a player's position technique—are generally a waste of time. For example, as a rule, drills that involve movements such as backpedaling and four-point bear crawling are inappropriate for defensive linemen. A coach should keep in mind that defensive linemen have two primary objectives—to avoid being knocked off the ball and to stay on their feet. In accomplishing these objectives, a defensive lineman never runs backward and rarely crawls on the ground. If a defensive lineman does get knocked to the ground, he should attempt to get to his feet as quickly as possible and find the ball. As a result, instead of developing his backpedaling technique or bear-crawl technique, a defensive lineman should be drilled on his lateral movement skills and on his technique in being able to quickly get up off the ground.

• *A drill should be conducted at a level of high intensity and should last for a relatively short duration.*

Technique drills, especially defensive line drills, should be designed so that the athlete moves quickly over a short period of time. Accordingly, defensive line coaches should employ drills that emphasize the intensity of movement, as opposed to such factors as how far a defensive lineman can run, how far the defensive lineman can push a sled, or how many dummy obstacles that linemen can clear. Rather, a defensive line coach should be more concerned with how fast a defensive lineman moves, how hard he hits the sled, and how quickly his feet move over the dummy obstacles. To a point, technique drills should not focus on the conditioning factor. Including conditioning as a secondary objective of a drill sometimes undermines the primary objective of a drill and destroys the opportunity to provide positive reinforcement of the athlete's ability to maintain his intensity level.

• *A drill should include a "fun" factor.*

To a point, defensive line drills should involve a measure of energy. As such, they should be designed so an athlete can easily get excited about the activity and want to excel during the drill. One of the most effective ways to interject a degree of enjoyment into a defensive line drill is to focus on some competitive aspect of the drill. For example, how far a particular player knocked the sled backward or how high he knocked a sled upward on his punch technique could be used as a quantitative basis to challenge the other defenders to beat or at least equal his accomplishments.

Regarding the need to introduce "fun" into their drills, some coaches feel that it is their responsibility to constantly chatter through a drill to create an atmosphere of excitement. It is important to keep in mind, however, that the endless repetition of "catch phrases" can actually be detrimental to the goal of establishing an atmosphere of electricity. While players of all levels tend to appreciate sincere verbal reinforcement, a coach who constantly blurts out the player's names or phrases and words such as "get there, get there" and "quick feet, quick feet" can easily foster an atmosphere of staleness and insincerity. In reality, an appropriate drill atmosphere can best be enhanced by a coach who moves with his players, stands near the drill, and calls them by name when he comments on a positive aspect of their performance. To a point, a coach should discipline himself to avoid unduly commenting on a player who is exhibiting incorrect techniques during a drill. Players who execute the drill in the manner desired should be pointed out. Players who are unable to master the essential skills involved in a drill should not be required to endlessly repeat the drill—either to punish (i.e., motivate) him or to make him improve his techniques. Instead, such players should be given extra work after practice. The point to remember is that an atmosphere of electricity and excitement cannot be maintained when giving endless repetitions to athletes who simply need more individualized instruction.

One other important coaching point with regard to injecting the "fun" factor into defensive line drills is the fact that such drills should be constantly reviewed and revised as necessary (i.e., as often as possible). While some skills are "daily must" drills (i.e., drills that should be conducted on a daily basis), a coach should carefully examine all of his drills and develop modifications and variations to each drill to keep it as "fresh" as possible. A drill should never be allowed to become stale to the players. If a drill becomes drudgery to the players, it should be discarded—even if it was a relatively great drill. In turn, a completely new drill should be developed to practice the same skill. Continually developing new drills or inserting fresh components into existing drills to help to keep them fun and challenging for the players is an essential task that should be undertaken by all defensive line coaches.

• *A drill should finish with a simulated tackle.*

Whenever appropriate, each repetition of a defensive line drill should finish with a simulated tackle on a dummy, sled, or another lineman. A defensive lineman should be trained to not only execute his technique properly, but also to finish each play by getting to the ball and making the tackle. While a coach doesn't want to place undue emphasis on conditioning during his technique drills, he should take care that his defensive line drills don't take on a "two-steps-and-stop" quality. He must encourage his players to execute the proper technique, then release and fly to the ball with reckless abandon. In this regard, one of the best ways to develop a player's total technique is to have him finish each repetition of a drill with a simulated tackle. As a variation, recovery technique should be taught at the end of the drills.

Note: The 18 drills presented in this chapter are designed to develop and refine many of the essential skills that a defensive lineman should possess. A detailed overview of drills for rushing the passer is provided by three Coaches Choice videos done by John Levra, titled *Pass Rush Fundamentals and Techniques, Pass Rush Games and Stunts,* and *Pass Rush Drills.*

Drill #1: Get-Off

Objective: To develop the ability of a defensive lineman to take a "big first step"

Equipment Needed: Football

Description: The players form two three- or four-man lines, depending on the front. The defensive linemen who play on the defensive left form the left line, while the defensive linemen who play on the defensive right form the right line. The coach kneels between the players and moves the ball. On the movement of the ball, the defensive linemen get off on the movement and sprint five to 10 yards ahead. Each player should push off his front foot and take a big first step as he explodes from his stance.

Coaching Points:
- The coach should check the stance of each player.
- The coach should provide input to each player on the length of his first step.
- The coach can have an entire defensive unit (e.g., first unit, second unit) perform the drill together.
- The coach should use a hard cadence and mix up the count if he needs to emphasize that aspect during this drill.

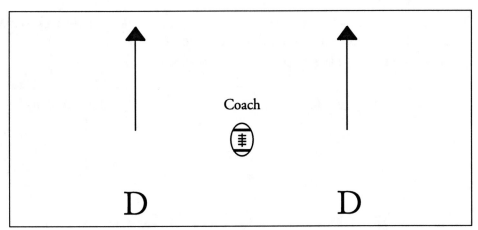

Diagram 7-1. The get-off drill

Drill #2: Throw the Hands

Objective: To develop the ability of a defensive lineman to perform the throwing-the-hands technique

Equipment Needed: Football, hand shields, form-tackling dummy

Description: The players form two lines. The defensive linemen who play on the defensive left form the left line, while the defensive linemen who play on the defensive right form the right line. A teammate who is holding a hand shield just above his knee stands in front of each defensive lineman. The coach kneels between the players and moves the ball. On the movement of the ball, each defensive lineman gets off on the movement and throws his hands into the hand shield. The defensive lineman strikes the shield with the heels of his hands and drives the shield upward. The defensive lineman drives the shield-holder backward for two or three steps, then releases and sprints to a stand-up tackling dummy located at a point three yards to his outside. The defensive lineman should then execute a form tackle on the dummy.

Coaching Points:
- The coach should check the stance of each player.
- The coach should provide input to each player on the length of his first step.
- The player should push off his front foot and take a big first step as he explodes from his stance.
- The coach should emphasize the explosive punch of the hands and check to make sure that the hand shield is being driven upward from the punch.
- The drill may be done live by players wearing shoulder pads.

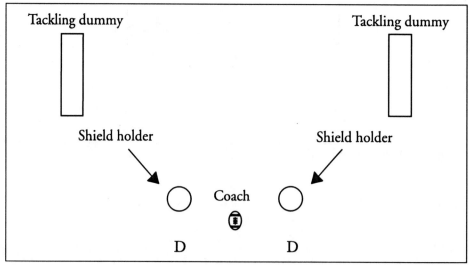

Diagram 7-2. Throw the hands drill

Drill #3: Squeeze the Down Block

Objective: To develop the 3-technique lineman's skill in playing a down block

Equipment Needed: Football, hand shield

Description: The players form two lines. The defensive linemen who play on the defensive left form the left line, while the defensive linemen who play on the defensive right form the right line. A teammate stands in front of each defensive lineman and squats so that he holds the shield just above his knee. Each line alternates after each repetition so that the coach can observe the technique of each player. After the coach gives the ready signal, the shield-holder goes inside on a down block angle, while holding the shield on his outside arm. On the initial movement of the shield-holder, the defensive lineman gets off and throws his hands into the hand shield. The defensive lineman should strike the shield with the heel of his inside hand and drive the shield upward. The defensive lineman should squeeze with the shield-holder for two steps, keeping his outside arm free and his shoulders square.

Coaching Points:
- The player should push off his front foot and take a big first step as he explodes from his stance.
- The coach should stand to the inside of the shield-holder and behind the line of scrimmage, so that he can see the eyes of the defensive lineman.
- The drill may be done live by players wearing shoulder pads.

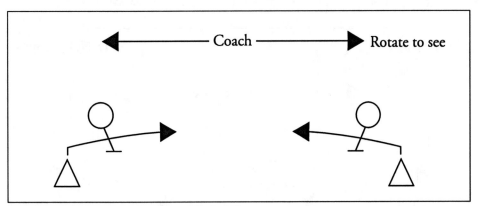

Diagram 7-3. Squeeze the down block drill

Drill #4: Beat the Hook Block

Objective: To develop the ability of a 3-technique lineman to defeat a hook block.

Equipment Needed: Football, hand shield, form-tackling dummy

Description: The players form two lines. The defensive linemen who play on the defensive left form the left line, while the defensive linemen who play on the defensive right form the right line. A teammate stands in front of the defensive lineman and squats so that he holds the hand shield just above his knee. Each line alternates after each repetition so that the coach can observe the technique of one player at a time. After the coach gives the ready signal, the shield-holder attacks the defensive lineman's outside shoulder, while holding the shield in his inside hand. On the movement of the shield-holder, the defensive lineman gets off and throws his hands into the hand shield. The defensive lineman should strike the shield with the heels of his hands and drive the shield upward. He should work to maintain outside leverage—keeping his outside arm free and his shoulders square. The defensive lineman should fight down the line of scrimmage to form tackle a dummy position on the line of scrimmage approximately seven yards outside of the starting point.

Coaching Points:
- The player should push off his front foot and take a big first step as he explodes out of his stance.
- The player should use his inside arm to rip across the face of the hook blocker as he separates to make the form tackle.
- The drill could also be performed by live players wearing shoulder pads.

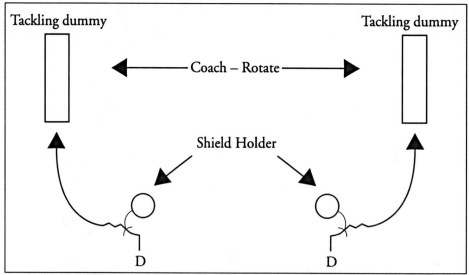

Diagram 7-4. Beat the hook block drill

Drill #5: Beat the Scoop Block

Objective: To develop the ability of a defensive lineman to defeat a scoop block

Equipment Needed: Football, two hand shields, form-tackling dummy

Description: The players form one line. The drill should be structured so that the defensive linemen who play on the defensive left get their repetitions from the left side of the ball, while the defensive linemen who play on the defensive right get their repetitions from the right side of the ball. Two teammates align as offensive linemen in cheated splits. Each player who simulates an offensive lineman holds a hand shield in his outside hand and assumes a three-point stance with the inside arm down. On the movement of the ball, the shield-holders run a scoop path to the inside. The outermost blocker attempts to sweep his outside arm and hand shield across the defender's face. The defensive lineman gets off on the movement and throws his hands to the primary blocker. The defensive lineman should flatten his path to the inside and use his outside-shoulder and forearm-flipper technique to ricochet off the hand shield of the outside blocker. The defensive lineman should fight down the line of scrimmage to form tackle a dummy positioned on the line of scrimmage approximately seven yards inside of the starting point.

Coaching Points:
- Each player should push off his front foot and take a big first step as he explodes out of his stance and gets his hat in the crack.
- The coach can use a string attached to a ball so that he can jerk the ball from a distance for the movement key and so that he can observe from a position relatively clear of the action. The players can also go on the first sound for more repetitions.
- The drill can also be performed live by players wearing shoulder pads.

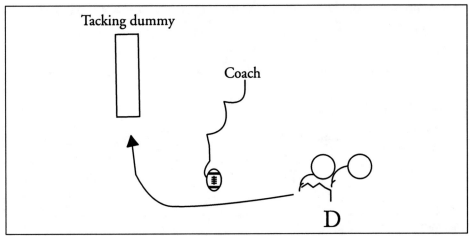

Diagram 7-5. Beat the scoop block drill

Drill #6: Jerk and Punch

Objective: To develop the ability of a defensive lineman to properly execute a swim move

Equipment Needed: None

Description: Two players stand facing each other at an arm's distance apart. One player assumes the role of an offensive dropback pass protector, while the other player acts as a defensive pass rusher. The offensive player lines up in a two-point football ready position, with his head back and his knees bent. He places his hands on the numbers on the defensive lineman. The defensive lineman is positioned in the correct posture for initiating a hands-on rushing move, such as a swim. The defensive lineman places one of his hands near the triceps of each arm of the blocker. The defensive lineman then quickly pulls downward on one of the blocker's shoulders in an attempt to depress the blocker's shoulder. At that moment, the defender uses his opposite arm and hand to punch over the head and depressed shoulder of the blocker. As the defender's arm punches over the blocker's depressed shoulder, the defender's foot that corresponds to the side of the punching hand quickly swings across his body and plants in a near heel-to-toe relationship beside the blocker's foot. The defensive lineman then freezes in that position and checks the positioning of his swing foot in relation to the blocker's foot. When his foot swing is completed, the defensive lineman should have gained an upfield advantage on the blocker. The drill continues for several repetitions to each side. The players then exchange roles.

Coaching Points:
- The defender should keep his thumbs up when he grabs the back of the blocker's upper arm. Keeping the thumbs up not only makes the grip stronger, but it also helps a defender prevent his hands from being pushed away by a blocker.
- The defender should snap his swing knee across the body of the blocker to plant his swing foot.

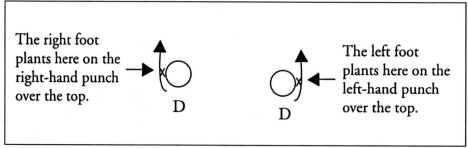

Diagram 7-6. Jerk and punch drill

Drill #7: Rip

Objective: To develop the ability of a defensive lineman to properly execute a rip move

Equipment Needed: None

Description: Two players stand facing each other at an arm's distance apart. One player assumes the role of an offensive dropback pass protector, while the other player acts as defensive pass rusher. The offensive player assumes a two-point football ready position, with his head back and his knees bent. He places his hands on the numbers of the defensive lineman. The defensive lineman assumes the correct posture for initiating a hands-on pass-rushing move, such as a push-pull or a swim. The defensive lineman places one of his hands near the triceps of each arm of the blocker. Releasing one arm of the blocker, the defensive lineman then rips his off-hand underneath the opposite armpit of the blocker. The rip is made in the manner of a violent uppercut punch. As the punch is made across the blocker's body, the foot of the defender that corresponds to the side of his punching hand quickly swings across his body and plants in a near heel-to-toe relationship beside the blocker's foot. The defensive lineman then freezes in that position and checks the positioning of his swing foot in relation to the blocker's foot. When the rip is completed, the defensive lineman should have gained an upfield advantage on the blocker. The drill should continue for several repetitions to each side before the players exchange roles.

Coaching Points:
- The defender should keep his thumbs up when he grabs the back of the blocker's upper arm. Keeping the thumbs up not only makes the grip stronger, but it also helps a defender prevent his hands from being pushed away by a blocker.
- The defender should push with the blocker's shoulder backward with his on-hand, as he uses his off-hand to rip across the blocker's body.

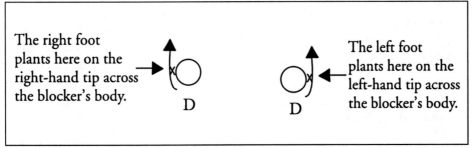

Diagram 7-7. Rip drill

Drill #8: Push-Pull

Objective: To develop the ability of a defensive lineman to properly execute a push-pull move

Equipment Needed: Form-tackling dummy

Description: Two players stand facing each other at an arm's distance apart. One player assumes the role of an offensive dropback pass protector, while the other player acts as a defensive pass rusher. The offensive player lines up in a two-point football ready position, with his head back and his knees bent. He places his hands on the numbers of the defensive lineman. The defensive lineman assumes the correct posture for initiating a hands-on pass-rushing move, such as a push-pull or a swim. The defensive lineman places one of his hands near the triceps of each arm of the blocker. Using both arms, the defensive lineman then shoves the blocker backward so that the blocker's weight shifts backward. The defensive lineman immediately follows the push move with a pull move by jerking the blocker's shoulders forward. He then finishes the move by releasing one arm of the blocker and ripping his off-hand underneath the opposite armpit of the blocker. The rip is made in the manner of a violent uppercut punch. As the punch is made across the blocker's body, the defender's foot that corresponds to the side of his punching hand quickly swings across his body and plants in a near heel-to-toe relationship beside the blocker's foot. The defensive lineman then clears the blocker and continues to rush a stand-up dummy positioned as a passing quarterback. The drill continues for several repetitions to each side before the players exchange roles.

Coaching Point:
- The offensive player should exaggerate the imbalance created by the defender's push-pull technique to help the defender develop the mechanics of the move.

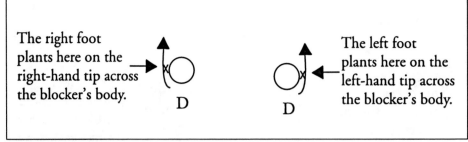

Diagram 7-8. Push-pull drill

Drill #9: Back Door

Objective: To develop the ability of a defensive lineman to play the fold and "U" block by going back door and pursuing flat down the line of scrimmage

Equipment Needed: Two cylinder dummies, two hand shields, two form-tackling dummies

Description: Three blockers align on the line of scrimmage. A defender is positioned across from the blockers. Two cylinder dummies are positioned behind the line of scrimmage. For continuity purposes, the movement key is on a snap count for the three offensive blockers and on the movement of the blockers for the defender. The defensive player aligns in one of the three alignment techniques on the middle blocker. The coach hand signals directions to the players and gives the count to the offensive blockers. If a fold block is signaled, the defender will attack using a big first step and will dip his inside shoulder to go back door. The primary blocker will pull to the inside, as the defender gets in his hip pocket flat down the line of scrimmage. If a "U" block is signaled, the defensive player will attack using a big first step and will dip his outside shoulder to go back door. The primary blocker will pull to the outside on the "U" block. The defender will get in the primary blocker's hip pocket to pursue flat down the line of scrimmage. The coach alternates fold blocking and "U" blocking as the defender becomes proficient at the back-door technique. The angle blockers hold a hand shield in the hand that is nearest the defender and use it for a blocking surface.

Coaching Points:
- The player should finish the drill by sprinting to the form-tackling dummy that is positioned seven yards to either side of the starting point on the line of scrimmage.
- The drill can also be conducted live by players wearing shoulder pads.

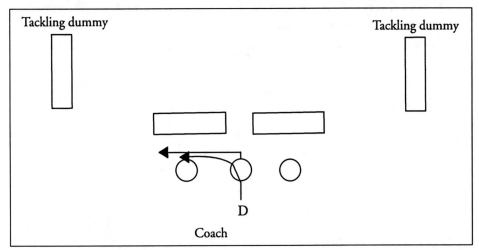

Diagram 7-9. Back door drill

Drill #10: Two-Man Sled Attack

Objective: To develop the ability of a defensive lineman to throw his hands in an upward thrust

Equipment Needed: Football with a string, two-man sled

Description: Two defensive linemen kneel approximately 18 inches away from the pad of the sled. The defensive linemen should sit back on their heels, keep their upper bodies erect, and bow their necks so that their heads are back. The ball is jerked by a string attachment so that the coach is able to stand back from the drill and observe the hand placement, elbow angle, and hip snap of the defenders. On movement of the ball, the defenders violently throw their hands into the pad of the sled. Initially, such a blow is made without the defenders employing hip or leg extension for several repetitions. The drill then progresses to a point where the defenders are required to strike a blow and follow with their hips, knocking the sled backward so that each defender is able to "lay out" in front of the sled after throwing the blow. The players then immediately recover and get ready for another repetition.

Coaching Points:
- When laying out to deliver a blow, the player's body should contact the ground in the following sequence: lower thigh, upper thigh, belt line, navel, and finally, the upper abdomen. Observing the player's actual sequence of contacting the ground can provide the coach with a relatively foolproof read of whether the athlete is properly developing his technique.
- The sled should fly upward and outward. No player or coach should stand on the sled. The sled should be kept as light as possible to increase the psychological benefit of the sled being knocked up in the air.
- The players should attack the sled with the heels of their hands (thumbs up), use a chuck grasp, and keep their elbows in.

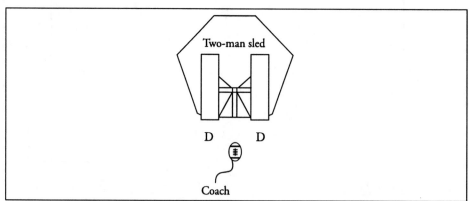

Diagram 7-10: Two-man sled attack drill

Drill #11: Two-Man Sled Attack–Finish

Objective: To develop the ability of a defensive lineman to attack, recover, and sprint to tackle an opponent

Equipment Needed: Football with a string, two-man sled (if possible, a stiff, older-style sled should be used)

Description: Two defensive linemen align in their proper three-point stance—approximately 18 inches away from the pad of the sled. The ball is jerked by a string attachment that enables the coach to stand back from the drill and observe the hand placement, the elbow angle, and the hip snap of the defenders. On the ball's movement, the defenders violently throw their hands into the pads of the sled. They then extend their hips and drive the sled in a quick burst of churning footwork. The coach quickly sounds his whistle. At that point, the players execute an outward seat roll and get up to sprint as fast as possible to the form-tackling dummy.

Coaching Points:
- The sled should fly upward and outward. No player or coach should stand on the sled. The sled should be kept as light as possible to increase the psychological benefit of being able to knock the sled up into the air.
- The players should attack the sled with the heel of their hands (thumbs up), use a chuck grasp, and keep their elbows in.
- A competitive factor can easily be incorporated into the drill by having the coach point out to the drill participants how far the sled flew when their teammates struck it on the previous repetition. If each successive group attempts to better the previous group's efforts, the drill can become quite enjoyable.

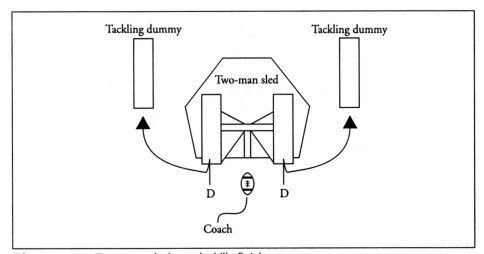

Diagram 7-11. Two-man sled attack drill—finish

Drill #12: Anchor Sled Shuffle

Objective: To develop the ability of a defensive lineman to demonstrate the strike-shuffle-strike skill needed to play down the line of scrimmage

Equipment Needed: A five-man sled anchored by metal stakes

Description: A single column of players start the drill by lining up in front of one station at the end of the sled. Upon a signal from the coach, the player in front of the sled strikes the pad and then moves to his right to get into position to hit the next pad. At that point, the next player in line moves up to strike the sled and to become part of the procession of players moving down the line (i.e., the sled). When moving to their right, the players keep the right foot back and punch each pad with both hands. The hands should strike the pad so that the thumbs are placed up. Each player should strike and slide, while keeping his back straight and his head back. As he engages in the drill, each player should use his trail leg (i.e., his left leg) to step into the blow delivery as he moves to the right. His elbows should be kept close to his body. The line reverses directions after each player completes his repetitions down one side of the sled.

Coaching Points:
- Because the sled is anchored, the players should emphasize the upward strike of the sled and attempt to make the pad rise into the air.
- The players in position in front of the pads on the sled should work together so that they strike the sled simultaneously.

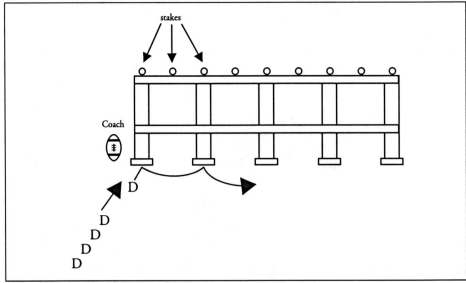

Diagram 7-12. Anchor sled shuffle drill

Drill #13: Anchor Sled "Shoulder Attack"

Objective: To develop the ability of a defensive lineman to deliver a shoulder blow and "fit" to the blocker with his hat in the crack

Equipment Needed: Football with a string, five-man sled anchored by metal stakes

Description: A player is positioned in front of each pad on the anchor sled. All of the players align in the same technique—either a 1 technique or a 3 technique. To cue movement, the coach uses a ball with a string attached. On the movement of the ball, the players get off on the ball and use a shoulder-blow delivery technique to attack the pad. The players should hold their positions on the sled after completing the forearm- and shoulder-blow delivery so that the coach can evaluate their landmark. Each player's landmark should be a tightly fitted headgear to the pad of the sled. His earhole should be in contact with the side of the pad, his neck should be bowed, and his eyes should be looking up. He should be in a "football position" on the sled—knees bent, back straight, and hips flexed, with feet set shoulder-width apart underneath the body. When the coach gives the command to release, the players should reset and change their technique alignment.

Coaching Points:
- Because the sled is anchored, the players should emphasize the upward strike of the sled and attempt to make the pad rise into the air.
- The players actively involved in the drill at any given time should work together so that they strike the sled simultaneously.
- Each defensive lineman should strike the pad with his wrist positioned so that his palm faces his chest and his thumb points up.
- The coach should alternate standing in front of the sled and behind the sled to check the ability of each player to adhere to the proper technique.

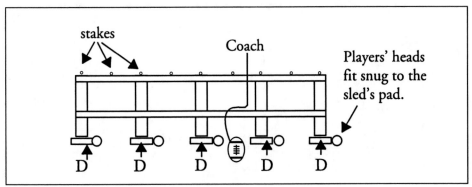

Diagram 7-13. Anchor sled "shoulder attack" drill

Drill #14: Anchor Sled "Hands Attack"

Objective: To develop the ability of a defensive lineman to deliver a blow with his hands and "fit" to the blocker with his hat in the crack

Equipment Needed: Football with a string, five-man sled anchored by metal stakes

Description: A player is positioned in front of each pad on the anchor sled. All of the players align in the same technique—either a 1 technique or a 3 technique. To cue movement, the coach uses a ball with a string attached. On the movement of the ball, the players get off on the ball and use a hands-blow delivery method to attack the pad. The players should hold their positions on the sled after striking the pad and locking out their arms, so that the coach can evaluate their landmark. The player's neck should be bowed and his eyes should be looking up. When the players use the hands-blow delivery technique, the head should not fit tightly to the pad (since the head will be away from the pad because of the lock-out of the arms). Even when using his hands, the player's head should remain on a line intersecting the side of the pad—just further back from the pad. He should be in a "football position" on the sled—knees bent, back straight, and hips flexed, with feet set should-width apart underneath the body. After the coach gives the command to release, the players should reset and change their technique alignment.

Coaching Points:
- Because the sled is anchored, the players should emphasize the upward strike of the sled to make the pad rise into the air.
- The players actively involved in the drill should work together so that they strike the sled simultaneously.
- When using the hands blow-delivery method, the defensive lineman should strike the pad with the heels of his hands. His fingers should be curled inward slightly and his elbows should be within the plane of his shoulders.

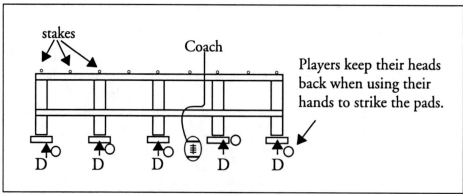

Diagram 7-14. Anchor sled "hands attack" drill

Drill #15: Quick Feet Shuffle

Objective: To develop the ability of a defensive lineman to move laterally with quick feet

Equipment Needed: Four low-profile footwork dummies, one form-tackling dummy, football

Description: Four footwork dummies are positioned on the ground, approximately 18 inches apart, as shown in Diagram 7-15. A defender assumes a football ready position with his head up, feet shoulder-width apart, knees bent, hips flexed, and back at a 45-degree or smaller angle to the ground. The player starts at one end of the line of dummies. In response to a movement signal by the coach, the defensive player shuffles through the dummies. Upon clearing the last dummy, the player accelerates to attack the tackling dummy and executes a form tackle. The player should lead with the foot that corresponds to the direction in which he is moving (e.g., if he is moving left, his left foot should lead over the dummies). His feet should not cross over as he moves laterally through the dummies. The player should keep himself in a ready position, with his eyes on the coach as he moves through the dummies. His hands should hang at his knees, nearly brushing the top of the dummies as he passes over them.

Coaching Points:
- The coach should encourage the players to look at him as they shuffle through the dummies.
- The coach should encourage the players to stay low as they shuffle through the dummies.
- Folded towels may be used in place of the footwork dummies.

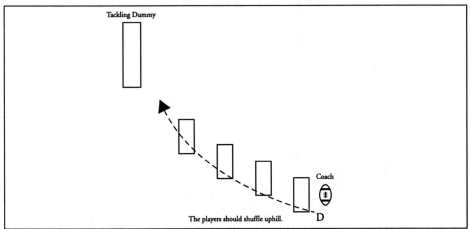

Diagram 7-15. Quick feet shuffle drill

Drill #16: Shuffle-Redirect

Objective: To develop the ability of a defensive lineman to plant off his lead foot and direct his movement to gain playside leverage on the ballcarrier

Equipment Needed: Four low-profile footwork dummies, one form-tackling dummy, football

Description: Four footwork dummies are positioned on the ground, approximately 18 inches apart, as shown in Diagram 7-16. The tackling dummy is positioned six to seven yards from the first dummy. A player assumes the football ready position—neck bowed, head up, feet shoulder-width apart, knees bent, shoulders back, back flat, and hips slightly flexed. The player starts at one end of the line of dummies. In response to a movement signal from the coach, the defensive player shuffles through the dummies. After the player's lead foot clears the last dummy, he plants and pushes off his lead foot to redirect and accelerate to form tackle the tackling dummy.

Coaching Points:
- The coach should encourage the players to look at him as they shuffle through the dummies.
- The coach should encourage the players to stay low as they shuffle through the dummies.
- Folded towels may be used in place of the dummies.
- The difficulty of the drill can be increased by having the players plant and redirect on a movement cue from the coach.

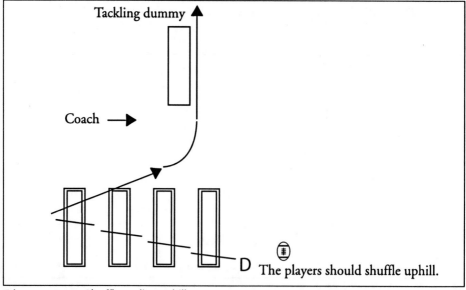

Diagram 7-16. Shuffle-redirect drill

Drill #17: Big Red Shuffle

Objective: To develop the ability of a defensive lineman to use his hands to play off a cut blocker and pressure the dash pass

Equipment Needed: Big red ball

Description: The big red ball is a coaching aide that is approximately 42 inches in diameter. (Note: One of the more common brands of balls is red). The ball's surface is textured with slight bumps so that the ball is more easily controlled by the coach and the player. The drill begins by having the coach roll the big red ball at the lineman's outside leg. The player shuffles to the outside and keeps his outside foot back as he focuses on the ball and strikes it with the heel of his hands to knock it back to the coach. The player then returns to the starting position. The coach pushes the ball toward the defender's outside leg for several repetitions. Players who play on the right side should work with their right foot back, and vice versa.

Coaching Points:
- The coach should encourage each player to shift his focus to the ball as he strikes the ball. Once the player strikes the ball, he should again focus on the coach.
- The drill can be conducted in a more gamelike condition by requiring the defender to move (i.e., work) laterally, thereby simulating his movement reaction to low cut blocks aimed at his outside thigh.

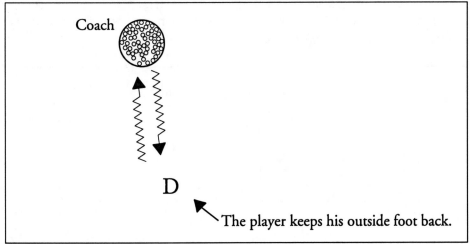

Diagram 7-17. Big Red shuffle drill

Drill #18: Form Tackling

Objective: To develop the ability of a defensive lineman to tackle properly

Equipment Needed: Hand shield

Description: Two players face each other from a distance of four to five feet. The player designated as a ballcarrier holds a hand shield in front of his chest with both hands. The shield holder moves to his right at a slow and controlled pace. The tackler mirrors the movement of the shield holder, closing the distance between them. The tackler should maintain the proper tackling position as he closes to the shield holder. To maintain the proper tackling position, the tackler should:

- Keep his eyes up
- Keep his neck bowed and his head back
- Pull his shoulders back so that his back is flat
- Set his feet shoulder-width apart
- Bend his knees and flex his hips so that his back lowers to the desired angle

The tackler's head should always be positioned behind the plane of his chest. The tackler should strike the shield with his chest and the front of his shoulders. His helmet's facebar should make only a very slight contact on the shield as he strikes upward through the shield. The tackler should use both of his arms to club upward under the shield holder's armpits, raking the arms of the shield holder upward. The tackler should bring his hands together as he hits "on a rise" through the shield holder. He should also churn his legs and squeeze the shield holder as he drives him backward for several steps. The tackler should be sure that his fingers are spread as he is grabbing the jersey of the ballcarrier.

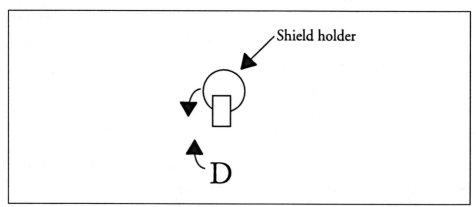

Diagram 7-18. Form tackling drill

Coaching Points:

- The coach should make sure that the tackler doesn't hit downward on the shield holder.
- The coach should not allow the tackler to drive the shield holder into the ground.
- The coach should strictly require the tackler to adhere to proper head positioning and should not allow the tackler to hit with his head leading his shoulders.
- The drill is best done in the following sequence: walk-through, half-speed, and three-quarters speed.
- The drill should never be done at full speed.
- After the tacklers have demonstrated the proper striking technique, the drill may be done in full gear, with a football replacing the shield.

8

Assessing Player Performance

One of the most invaluable assignments that can be undertaken by a defensive line coach is to responsibly assess the performance level of his position players. If conducted properly, such an assignment can help achieve a number of objectives, including the following:

- Measure that part of a defensive lineman's contribution to the team's effort that can be isolated
- Provide a coaching tool for improving future performance (i.e., produce a quantitative basis for what's going right and wrong)
- Provide defensive linemen with a measurable standard of performance
- Give defensive linemen a definitive goal of performance-related factors to shoot for
- Provide a coaching tool for assessing the relative effectiveness of a particular teaching or coaching technique that is currently being employed
- Facilitate putting specific parts of the team's mission statement into action (e.g., play aggressively on every play, play smart, win the turnover battle)

Sources of Performance Factors

As a general rule, assessing the performance of a defensive lineman involves identifying a laundry list of factors that can be used to appraise a player's on-field efforts and then evaluating how each player performs relative to each factor. Tables 8-1 and 8-2 provide examples of how the performance of defensive linemen might be quantitatively evaluated during a specific game or over the course of a season, respectively.

Item	Points	Description
Positives		
Sacks	4	Sack the quarterback
Nasty	3	Knock a blocker down
Knockdowns	2	Knock the quarterback down
Hits	2	Hit the quarterback while he is passing
Pressures	2	Apply pressure on the quarterback
TK loss	3	Make a tackle for a loss
TK	2	Tackle the ballcarrier
A. TK	1	Assist on a tackle
C. fumble	2	Cause a fumble
R. fumble	2	Recover a fumble
Clean move	2	Execute a clean move
Break up	2	Break up a pass attempt
Cept.	4	Intercept a pass
TD	10	Score a touchdown
Safety	6	Cause a safety
Negatives		
M.A.		Miss an assignment
Loaf		Fail to go all-out on the play
SOL		Get stuck on the line of scrimmage
OG		Get knocked to the ground
TMT		Allow the quarterback too much time on a pass play
O.S.		Go offside
Late T.O.		Take off late
Busted game		Allow a stunt to break down
No move		Fail to execute a move
2-gap		Get locked up
Missed tackle		Miss the tackle
Missed sack		Miss the sack
Too nice		Be too passive on a play
Production percentage		An index of the number of total net points earned divided by the total number of plays in which the player is in the game

Key for Tables 8-1 and 8-2

Opponent:_____ Date:_____ Name:_____

Total plays:_____ (+)s_____ (−)s_____ Production %_____

Production	Negatives	Improve on these

Production   **Negatives**   **Improve on these**

Sacks_____   M.A._____

Nasty_____   Loaf_____

Knockdowns_____   SOL_____

Hits_____   OG_____

Pressures_____   TMT_____

TK loss_____   O.S._____

TK_____   Late T.O._____

A. TK_____   Busted game_____

C. fumble_____   No move_____

R. fumble_____   2-gap_____

Clean move_____   Missed tackle_____

Break-up_____   Missed sack_____

Cept._____   Too nice_____

Touchdown_____

Safety_____

NET PT TOTAL_____   PRODUCTION %_____

Overall Evaluation _____

_____

_____

Team Defensive Stats

Passes attempted_____   Rushes_____

Sacks_____   Yards_____

Knockdowns_____   Average_____

Hits_____

Pressures_____

Nasty_____

Table 8-1. Single game rushmen analysis

Opponent: _____

Date: _____

Factor	Sacks	Nasty	KDs	Hits	PR	TK Loss	TK	AT	C.F.	R.F.	C.M.	B.Up	Cept.	TD	Safety	Pt. Total	Total Plays	Prod %
Assigned Due	(4)	(3)	(2)	(2)	(2)	(3)	(2)	(1)	(2)	(2)	(2)	(2)	(4)	(10)	(6)			
PLAYER																		
SHUGG																		
JOHN																		
JASON																		
D.A.																		
STALIN																		
DUANE																		
JERRY																		
TONY																		

Table 8-2. Entire season rushmen-production totals

With regard to assessing a player's performance level, one of the most important things that a defensive line coach can do is to carefully identify the specific aspects of performance to be evaluated. As such, these factors should generally meet several criteria, including the following:

- The factors must be perceived as important (e.g., quarterback sacks, tackles).
- The factors must be relevant to the position (e.g., quarterback pressures, nasties).
- The factors must be reliable (i.e., the item being measured would be measured the same way and would yield the same result from game to game).
- The factors should provide a fair and accurate basis for comparing different individuals with the same basic job responsibilities (e.g., comparing the performance of one particular defensive lineman with another).
- The factors must provide a useful basis for assessing performance.
- The factors must be relevant to the goals of the organization (both to the defensive team and to the entire squad).
- As a rule, the factors should be cut and dried (crystal clear versus subjective). Examples include the number of tackles for a loss, the number of fumble recoveries, etc.

Gathering and Applying the Assessment Data

Making a commitment to assessing the performance of his players and then deciding what factors to use to undertake such an assessment are only the initial steps that a defensive line coach must undertake in the process of evaluating his players. He must also determine how he is going to gather the performance-related data and what the collected data means.

As a rule, the technological advances in media tools available to coaches (e.g., digital video records and playback devices, CD-ROM players, laptop computers) have made the gathering of evaluative information and the sharing of that information with their players substantially easier. For example, a defensive line coach can watch and analyze game film and then transfer the information he collects to a basic spreadsheet program on his computer. Obviously, he can also record the information by hand, using the much more traditional method.

Once the data has been collected and transcribed, the defensive line coach needs to decide what application the data has to the situation at hand. At a minimum, he should share the information with his position players so that they have a valid, reliable basis for understanding whether they are performing up to expectations.

To gain a better grasp of the collective meaning of the performance evaluations, most coaches also attempt to weigh the various performance factors into a single

Opponent: **Skins** Date: **8-28** Name: **Phil**

Total plays: **25** (+)s **19** (−)s **6** Production % **76**

Production	**Negatives**	**Improve on these**
Sacks _____	M.A. _____	Recognize the
Nasty _____	Loaf _____	G-play in over.
Knockdowns _____	SOL ___ ✓ ___	Stay aligned on
Hits _____	OG ___ ✓ ___	TE in over
Pressures _____	TMT _____	bullets.
TK loss __ 1 __	O.S. _____	No Tiger away
TK __ 2 __	Late T.O. _____	from Sam
A. TK __ 2 __	Busted game _____	bullets.
C. fumble _____	No move _____	Find BC.
R. fumble _____	2-gap _____	
Clean move _____	Missed tackle _____	
Break-up _____	Missed sack _____	
Cept. _____	Too nice _____	

Touchdown _____

Safety _____

"We can improve a little this week in practice – Let's Get It Done"

NET PT TOTAL __ 9 __   PRODUCTION % __ 36 __

Overall Evaluation __ Quicker recognition of high-hat. __
Pass – better takeoff; move on ball. Footwork
& timing on stunts. Eliminate guessing on runs.

Team Defensive Stats

Passes attempted __ 26 __		Rushes __ 18 __	
Sacks __ 3 excellent ✓ __		Yards __ 77 __	
Knockdowns __ 1 __		Average __ 43 – too high ✓ __	
Hits __ 2 __			
Pressures __ 5 __			
Nasty __ 1 __			

Table 8-3. Defensive lineman's single-game performance analysis

Factor	Sacks	Nasty	KDs	Hits	PR	TK Loss	TK	AT	C.F.	R.F.	C.M.	B.Up	Cept.	TD	Safety	Pt. Total	Total Plays	Prod %
Assigned Due	(4)	(3)	(2)	(2)	(2)	(3)	(2)	(1)	(2)	(2)	(2)	(2)	(4)	(10)	(6)			
PLAYER																		
PHIL			2	1	2	1	3	2								21	51	41
SEAN M.						1		1								6	31	19
TED							2	3								7	36	19
BRUCE																		
MARCELLUS	1		1		2		4	6								18	52	35
SEAN P.					1		2									12	23	52
PAT					1			1								3	8	38

Table 8-4. All defensive linemen's production levels for a single game

assessment rating. In other words, by translating the numbers into a "rating," the coach is figuratively giving his players a "grade" on their performance. Table 8-3 illustrates how the efforts of a particular defensive lineman could be analyzed for a specific game, while Table 8-4 provides an overview of the productivity level for all of the defensive linemen for a given game. The resultant production percentages could then be applied to a rating scale that the coach deems appropriate. An example of a scale that could be used to assess the performance data in Tables 8-3 and 8-4 is presented in Table 8-5.

Production Percentage	Rating
Over 40%	Very good
26–40%	Good
16–25%	Average
15% or less	Below average

Table 8-5. Subjective rating scale for assessing the productivity percentage level of a defensive lineman.

About the Authors

John Levra retired from coaching after serving for 44 years in the profession. He finished his career as the defense line coach for the Buffalo Bills (five years). He served in the same position with the Minnesota Vikings for three years. For two years at the Denver Broncos, he was the offensive line coach. Prior to that experience, he coached the defensive line for the Chicago Bears for seven years. His first NFL position was as the running backs coach for the New Orleans Saints (five years). In 1980, he was the defensive line coach for the British Columbia Lions of the CFL. In his 15 years as a defensive line coach, his units averaged 46 sacks a season.

John spent seven years as a high school coach in Kansas before his college coaching career began at New Mexico Highlands as an assistant in 1966. He then became the Cowboys' head coach (1967–70) and posted the best coaching record (35-4-1) in school history. He was named the athletic director and head football coach at Stephen F. Austin University in 1971, where he established the second-best winning percentage in the school's history. In 1974, he moved to the University of Kansas, where he served as the Jayhawk's offensive coordinator for four seasons. He then accepted the same position at North Texas State for one season (1979).

John is a graduate of Pittsburg (KS) State, where he earned All-Central Intercollegiate Conference honors as a guard/linebacker. John is widely respected as one of the most outstanding "teachers" in the coaching profession. He is a much sought-after clinic speaker and has produced three best-selling instructional videos: *Pass Rush Fundamentals and Techniques, Pass Rush Games and Stunts,* and *Pass Rush Drills.* John and his wife, Rosie, have two children—Craig and Gina—and two grandchildren—twins Chase and Samantha.

James A. Peterson, Ph.D., FACSM, is a freelance writer who has authored 64 books and more than 200 published articles on a variety of coaching- and health-related subjects. Among the books he has helped write is *Bill Walsh: Finding the Winning Edge* with Bill Walsh and Brian Billick. A 1966 graduate of the University of California at Berkeley, Jim was a professor in the Department of Physical Education at the United States Military Academy at West Point (1971–90), before serving as the director of sports medicine for StairMaster Sports/Medical Products, Inc. (1990–95). Jim and his wife, Sue, reside in Monterey, California.